04

05
05

06

Before the
Best Interests of
the Child

So long as the child is part of a viable family, his own interests are merged with those of the other members. Only *after* the family fails in its function should the child's interests become a matter for state intrusion.

Before the Best Interests of the Child

JOSEPH GOLDSTEIN
Law School, Yale University

ANNA FREUD
Hampstead Child-Therapy Clinic

ALBERT J. SOLNIT
Child Study Center, Yale University

BURNETT BOOKS
in association with ANDRE DEUTSCH

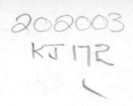

First published 1980 by Burnett Books Limited
in association with André Deutsch Limited
105 Great Russell Street London WC1

Reproduced, printed and bound in Great Britain by
Fakenham Press Limited, Fakenham, Norfolk

Paperback ISBN 0 233 97267 6

Hardback ISBN 0 233 97243 9

The quote from Agatha Christie's *An Autobiography* (see pages 221 and 222) is reproduced by permission of William Collins Sons & Co. Ltd. and of Dodd, Mead & Company. Copyright © 1977 by Agatha Christie Limited.

The abridged portion of the Committee of Inquiry report on Maria Colwell (see pages 144–82) is used with the permission of the Controller of Her Britannic Majesty's Stationery Office.

Contents

Preface

Readers may welcome some explanation why our three
authors reversed the sequence of events by tackling the
problems of *beyond* the best interests of the child
earlier than those that do come *before.* I can only sur-
mise that in 1973 the difficulties and mistakes surround-
ing child placement loomed so large and clamored so
insistently for solution that the questions when and for
what reasons these children find themselves at the mercy
of state disposition were pushed into the background.
However, as a listener to their discussions, I can testify
that even at the earlier date the points concerning protection for the parent-child relationship or the necessary
state intrusion into it were never absent from the
authors' minds. They were merely biding their time,
waiting for the already anticipated writing of a second
book.

Three authors, with different backgrounds and
on the basis of different experiences, cannot be expected
to tackle one and the same task in one and the same
manner. Again, a common language had to be devised to
satisfy the needs of two professions and of the lay
reader. In addition, however, agreement had to be
reached on a number of questions about the advantages
and disadvantages of state intervention, about the
merits and demerits of present-day parents in general,
and about the risk when parents are entrusted with the

final say in the serious matters of child rearing which used to be their sole prerogative in bygone days.

Discussion, no doubt, profited from previous experience. While mutual stimulation, pressure toward logical argumentation, and detailed exposition of points had remained the same, the participants knew more of each other's preferences, convictions, and idiosyncrasies. Accordingly, controversies, even though perhaps heated at the beginning, were solved more quickly and opinions merged more readily.

That every statement in this book has been weighed and doubted until confirmed by the working of three critical minds has, I trust, not detracted from the ease with which the book can be read and, therefore, from the readers' satisfaction and approval of the final formulations.

DOROTHY BURLINGHAM

Acknowledgments

Many individuals and several institutions have encouraged and facilitated our writing of this book. We wish to acknowledge our appreciation for their support.

For creative and demanding editorial assistance at all stages of writing and for helping to translate many of our proposals into statutory language: Sonja Goldstein.

For critical comment and elbow-to-elbow editorial help on various drafts of the manuscript: Lon Babby, David De Wolf, Steven Goldberg, Laird Hart, Paula Herman, Andrea Hirsch, Martha Minow, Donn Pickett.

For their thoughts: Bruce Ackerman, Robert Burt, Robert M. Cover, Owen Fiss, Paul Gewirtz, Barbara Grant, Lionel Hersov, Carol Larson, Howard A. Levine, Benjamin Lopata, Burke Marshall, Neil Peck, Sally Provence, Spiros Simitis, Martha Solnit, George Stroh, Jeff Thaler, Michael Wald, Andrew Watson, Stephen Wizner.

For encouragement and a setting in which to think at work: Abraham S. Goldstein and Harry Wellington, Deans, Law School, and Robert Berliner, Dean, School of Medicine, Yale University.

For careful and thoughtful editing and indexing: Lottie M. Newman.

For library assistance: Robert E. Brooks, Arthur

Charpentier, Gene Coakley, Isaiah Shein, Charles S. Smith.

For unstinting, cheerful, imaginative, and highly skilled preparation of the many drafts of manuscript: Liz Modena and Elizabeth H. Sharp.

For secretarial and photocopying assistance: Gina Bon, Albert Dingle, Gweneth Endfield, Russ Hentz, Walter Moriarty, Bea Nirenstein, Geraldine Perillo, Sophie Z. Powell, Ivy Weaver.

For generous and gratifying sustenance at all of our London meetings: Paula Fichtl.

For financial assistance (travel, study, and research grants): Elizabeth Dollard, The Ford Foundation, The Free Press, The Edna McConnell Clark Foundation, and the Office of Maternal and Child Health, DHEW.

Part One

The Problem, Our Convictions, and a Framework for Examining State Decisions to Intrude on Parent-Child Relationships

Chapter 1

The Problem and Our Convictions

When and why should a child's relationship to his parents become a matter of state concern? What must have happened to or in the life of a child before the state should be authorized to investigate, modify, or terminate an individual child's relationship with his parents, with his family? Considering what a child loses when he passes, even temporarily, from the personal authority of parents to the impersonal authority of the law, what grounds for placing a family under state scrutiny are reasonable? What can justify overcoming the presumption in law that parents are free to determine what is "best" for their children in accord with their own beliefs, preferences, and life-styles?

We did not ask these questions in *Beyond the Best Interests of the Child*.

In *Beyond the Best Interests of the Child* we restricted our inquiry almost exclusively to problems involving children already caught up in the legal system. We focused primarily on contested child placements "where the adults involved [including parents as well as state and private agency personnel] resort to the legal process for a resolution of their disputes."[1] We did not endorse existing grounds for coercive state intrusion on parent-child relationships, but generally took them as given. We did not consider, for example, whether the divorce of parents or the separation of unmarried parents should in themselves be grounds for the state to intervene—to decide not only who should have custody of their children but also to dictate the circumstances under which the newly established or reaffirmed legal relationships should be changed. Nor did we question the underlying justifications for invoking state authority to make placement decisions in such variously labeled proceedings as neglect, abandonment, abuse, delinquency, foster care, separation, and divorce. We sought merely to establish guidelines, based on psychoanalytic knowledge and reinforced by common sense, for assuring that the least detrimental placement would be selected by the least detrimental procedure for each child whose custody had become a matter of state concern.

The guidelines that we developed in *Beyond the Best Interests of the Child* rest on two convictions. First, we believe that a child's need for continuity of care by autonomous parents requires acknowledging that parents should generally be entitled to raise their children as they think best, free of state interference. This conviction finds expression in our preference for *minimum state intervention* and prompts restraint in defining justifications for coercively intruding on family relationships. Second, we believe that the child's well-being—not the parents', the family's, or the child care agency's—must be determinative once justification for state intervention has been established. Whether the protective shell of the family is already broken before the state intrudes, or breaks as a result of it, the goal of intervention must be to create or re-create a family for the child as quickly as possible. That conviction is expressed in our preference for *making a child's interests paramount* once his care has become a legitimate matter for the state to decide.

So long as a child is a member of a functioning family, his paramount interest lies in the preservation of his family. Thus, our preference for making a child's interests paramount is not to be construed as a justification in and of itself for intrusion.* Such a reading would ignore the advantages that accrue to children from a policy of minimum state intervention. The goal of every child placement, whether made automatically by birth certificate or more deliberately following direct intervention by administrative or court order, is the same. With the possible exception of the placement of violent juveniles, [2] it is to assure for each child membership in a family with at least one parent who wants him. It is to assure for each child and his parents an opportunity to maintain, establish, or reestablish psychological ties to each other free of further interruption by the state.

With these convictions and that common pur-

* "[T]he child's interest should be the paramount consideration once, *but not before,* a child's placement becomes the subject of official controversy" (*Beyond the Best Interests of the Child,* p. 105; emphasis supplied).

pose in mind, in *Beyond the Best Interests of the Child* we proposed and explained the following guidelines for determining the placement and process of placement for children whose custody becomes the subject of legal action:

> Placement decisions should safeguard the child's need for continuity of relationships.
> Placement decisions should reflect the child's, not the adult's, sense of time.
> Placement decisions must take into account the law's incapacity to supervise interpersonal relationships and the limits of knowledge to make long-range predictions.[3]

These guidelines, designed originally to pour content into the best interests standard—or what we call the least detrimental available alternative standard *— have substantial implications for defining justifications for state intrusion on family relationships.

The question we pose and seek to answer in this book is: "Why and under what circumstances should the state be authorized to invade family privacy and to overcome the presumption of parental autonomy?" But before attempting an answer, we focus first on the

---

* "The least detrimental alternative . . . is that specific placement and procedure for placement which maximizes, in accord with the child's sense of time and on the basis of short-term predictions given the limitations of knowledge, his or her opportunity for being wanted and for maintaining on a continuous basis a relationship with at least one adult who is or will become his psychological parent." [4]

meaning of and reasons for favoring a policy of minimum state intervention.

In the eyes of the law, to be a *child* is to be at risk, dependent, and without capacity or authority to decide free of parental control what is "best" for oneself. To be an *adult* is in law to be perceived as free to take risks, with the independent capacity and authority to decide what is "best" for oneself without regard to parental wishes.[5] To be an *adult who is a parent* is therefore to be presumed by law to have the capacity, authority, and responsibility to determine and to do what is "good" for one's children, what is "best" for the entire family.

As long ago as 1840 Jeremy Bentham observed:

> The feebleness of infancy demands a continual protection. Everything must be done for an imperfect being, which as yet does nothing for itself. The complete development of its physical powers takes many years; that of its intellectual faculties is still slower. At a certain age, it has already strength and passions, without experience enough to regulate them. Too sensitive to present impulses, too negligent of the future, such a being must be kept under an authority more immediate than that of the laws. . . .[6]

That "more immediate authority" is the authority of parents. They offer children protection and nurture, and introduce them to the demands and prohibitions as well as to the promises and opportunities of society. Charged with the duty of initiating the relationships of their children to the adult world and to its institutions, parents shelter their children from direct contact with the law by being their representatives before it.

By 1926 Freud brought a psychological dimension to Bentham's societal view of the "feebleness of infancy." He refers to "the long period of time during which the young of the human species is in a condition of helplessness and dependence," that "in comparison with . . . most animals, . . . it is sent into the world in a less finished state," and "the dangers of the external world have a greater importance for it." [7] He explains how this "biological factor" on the one hand burdens the parents with the full weight of responsibility for the survival and well-being of their offspring and, on the other hand, assures that the day-to-day ministering to the child's multiple requirements will turn the physical tie between them into a mutual psychological attachment.

Such constantly ongoing interactions between parents and children become for each child the starting point for an all-important line of development that leads toward adult functioning. What begins as the experience of physical contentment or pleasure that accompanies bodily care develops into a primary attachment to the person who provides it. This again changes into the wish for a parent's constant presence irrespective of physical wants. Helplessness requires total care and over time is transformed into the need or wish for approval and love. It fosters the desire to please by compliance with a parent's wishes. It provides a developmental base upon which the child's responsiveness to educational efforts rests. Love for the parents leads to identification with them, a fact without which impulse control and socialization would be deficient.[8] Finally, after the years of childhood comes the prolonged and in many ways painful adolescent struggle to attain a separate identity with physical, emotional, and moral self-reliance.[9]

These complex and vital developments require the privacy of family life under guardianship by parents who are autonomous. The younger the child, the greater is his need for them. When family integrity is broken or weakened by state intrusion, his needs are thwarted and his belief that his parents are omniscient and all-powerful is shaken prematurely. The effect on the child's developmental progress is invariably detrimental.[10] The child's need for safety within the confines of the family must be met by law through its recognition of family privacy as the barrier to state intrusion upon parental autonomy in child rearing.[11] These rights —parental autonomy, a child's entitlement to autonomous parents, and privacy—are essential ingredients of "family integrity." * "And the integrity of that life is something so fundamental that it has been found to draw to its protection the principles of more than one explicitly granted Constitutional right." [12]

Two purposes underlie the parents' right to be free of state intrusion. The first is to provide parents with an uninterrupted *opportunity* to meet the develop-

* We use the phrase "family integrity" rather than "family autonomy" to encompass the three liberty interests of direct concern to children (parental autonomy, the right to autonomous parents, and privacy) in order to avoid the confusion caused by using interchangeably "family autonomy" and "parental autonomy."

ing physical and emotional needs of their child so as to establish the familial bonds critical to every child's healthy growth and development. The second purpose, and the one on which the parental right must ultimately rest, is to safeguard the *continuing maintenance* of these family ties—of psychological parent-child relationships —once they have been established. The two purposes are usually fulfilled when the parental right is assigned at a child's birth simply on the basis of his biological tie to those who produce him. Likewise, for the adopted child, these purposes are usually met when the parental right is assigned simply on the basis of his legal tie to those who adopt him. But the assignment and recognition of parental rights do not guarantee that biological or adoptive parents will exercise them or that these parents will establish significant psychological ties to their child. Indeed, when parents abandon a child or when parents and children are separated "too long," their legal entitlement cannot and does not prevent the establishment of familial ties—psychological bonds —between their child and longtime substitute care-takers who have no parental right, no legal claim to raise him. These new relationships merit the same protection from state intervention as is accorded to the relationships in functioning biological and adoptive families.[13] Thus, rights which are normally secured over time by biological or adoptive parents may be lost by their failure to provide continuous care for their child and earned by those who do.*

---

* "As to the question of the right of the father to have the custody of his infant child, in a general sense it is true. But this is not on account of any absolute right of the father, but for the bene-

Put somewhat differently, two stages in the parent-child relationship generally define the right of family integrity that deserves recognition and protection from interruption by the state. The first is the stage at which the *opportunity* for the development of psychological ties between parent and child exists; the right usually comes about through a child's being placed with natural parents at birth, or through legally sanctioned adoption. These opportunities merit protection from state intrusion because it is only through continuous nurture of the child within the privacy of the family that the second stage can be reached. At that stage, primary psychological ties between parent and child have been established and require for their *maintenance* continuous nurture free of state intrusion. The liberty interest in these familial bonds, including bonds established between children and longtime fostering adults who are not their parents, has not yet been clearly perceived or firmly established in law. It is as deserving of recognition and protection as is the first stage, normally associated with biological reproduction or with adoption.[15]

Beyond these biological and psychological justifications for protecting parent-child relationships and promoting each child's entitlement to a permanent place in a family of his own, there is a further justification for a policy of minimum state intervention. It is that the law does not have the capacity to supervise the

---

fit of the infant, the law presuming it to be for his interest to be under the nurture and care of his natural protector, both for maintenance and education." Chief Justice Story in *United States* v. *Green*, 26 F. Cas. 30, 31 (C.C.R.I. 1824) (No. 15, 256).[14]

fragile, complex interpersonal bonds between child and parent.[16] As *parens patriae* the state is too crude an instrument to become an adequate substitute for flesh and blood parents. The legal system has neither the resources nor the sensitivity to respond to a growing child's ever-changing needs and demands. It does not have the capacity to deal on an individual basis with the consequences of its decisions, or to act with the deliberate speed that is required by a child's sense of time. Similarly, the child lacks the capacity to respond to the rulings of an impersonal court or social service agencies as he responds to the demands of personal parental figures. Parental expectations, implicit and explicit, become the child's own. However, the process by which a child converts external expectations, guidance, commands, and prohibitions into the capacity for self-regulation and self-direction does not function adequately in the absence of emotional ties to his caretakers.

A policy of minimum coercive intervention by the state thus accords not only with our firm belief as citizens in individual freedom and human dignity, but also with our professional understanding of the intricate developmental processes of childhood.

To recognize how critical are the developmental stages and how essential are autonomous parents for the protection of their children is also to recognize that parents may fail. Not all parents are able or willing to safeguard their child against the succession of risks which bedevil development from dependent infancy to independent adulthood. They may fail to protect their child from unwarranted risk. Family privacy may become a cover for exploiting the inherent inequality between adult and child.[17] It may prevent detection of the uncontrolled expression of both the unconscious and conscious hatred some parents have for their children. Family privacy ceases to benefit the child and becomes a threat to his well-being, to his safety, and occasionally to his life. Those dangers justify state intervention.

Yet, to acknowledge that some parents, whether biological, adoptive, or longtime foster, may threaten the well-being of their children is not to suggest that state legislatures, courts, or administrative agencies can always offer such children something better, and compensate them for what they have missed in their own homes. By its intrusion the state may make a bad situation worse; indeed, it may turn a tolerable or even a good situation into a bad one.

The intact family offers the child a rare and continuing combination of elements to further his growth: reciprocal affection between the child and two, or at least one, caretaking adult; the feeling of being wanted and therefore valued; and the stimulation of inborn capacities. Available alternatives too often fail to offer the whole series, and accordingly leave one or the other part of the child's personality without developmental support.[18] Recognition of these shortcomings should alert the law to ask in every case whether removal from an unsatisfactory home is the beneficial measure it purports to be.

Identifying children in serious jeopardy requires more than the vague and subjective language of "change of conditions of custody" in divorce statutes and "denial of proper care" in neglect and abuse statutes that give administrative agencies and courts unguided discretion to supervise and even terminate parent-child relationships. Such statutes must be revised to protect all families—poor and well-to-do, minority and majority, biological, adoptive, and longtime foster. They must provide these ongoing relationships with safeguards from unwarranted state-sponsored interruptions. They must prevent judges, lawyers, social workers, and others from imposing their personal, even if professional, preferences upon unwilling parents. To that end we ask and seek to answer:

> What ought to be established and by what procedure *before* the "best interests of the child" can be invoked over the rights of parents to autonomy, the rights of children to autonomous parents, and the rights of both parents and children to family privacy?

Chapter 2

The Framework

What should be the role of law in protecting children from parental exploitation and both children and parents from exploitation by the state? In other words, under a policy of minimum intervention, what should the law require *before* the best interests of a child may become a matter of state determination? These questions call for identification of those circumstances that should justify invading the right of parents and their children to feel at home with one another [1] and to be secure in their persons and dwellings.[2]

We postpone substantive answers to our questions (a) until we have described and explained the requirements that *any* grounds for coercive state intrusion on parent-child relationships must meet; and (b) until we have identified the points of decision and clarified their functions in applying any ground for intervention to a specific family.

FAIR WARNING AND POWER RESTRAINT

The law has given two distinct responses to the question, "What should justify substituting the state's judgment for that of parents with regard to the care of a particular child?" The first has been to set relatively precise limits on parental judgment concerning matters about which there is a clear societal consensus. For example, parents are not free to send their children into the labor market or to refuse to let them attend school or be immunized against certain contagious diseases.[3] Legislative enactments like those concerned with child labor, compulsory education, and immunization are infringements upon parental autonomy which give parents fair warning of what constitutes a breach of their child care responsibilities and provide advance notice of the extent of the state's power to intervene. In thus defining the authority to intrude in precise terms, legislatures also restrict the power of administrative agencies and courts to breach the state's general commitment to family privacy and parental autonomy.

The second form which legislative responses take, and the one on which we focus in this book, sets relatively vague and imprecise limits upon authority to intrude and thus fails to provide fair warning. Those statutes concern child care matters about which there is no clear societal consensus. They delegate to administrators, prosecutors, and judges the power to invade privacy almost at will—"the authority of *ad hoc* decision, which is in its nature difficult if not impossible to hold to account."[4] Though everyone may agree that children ought not to be "neglected" or "abused" or that their "best interests" should be served, there is little agreement about the meaning of these terms.[5] For example, legislative enactments which simply make "denial of proper care" the standard for investigating or determining "neglect," and "significant change of circumstances" the standard for modifying custody after divorce, provide neither meaningful advance warning to parents nor adequate guidance for courts or administrative agencies.

This second form of legislation, unlike the first form, invests judges and state agency personnel as *parens patriae* with almost limitless discretion in areas generally under the exclusive control of parents. Such legislation is used to justify the *ad hoc* creation of standards of intervention in case-by-case determinations to investigate, supervise, and supervene parental judgments. It invites the exploitation of parents and children by state officials. Acting in accord with their own personal child-rearing preferences, officials have been led to discriminate against poor, minority, and other disfavored families.[6]

To reduce unwarranted intrusions on family integrity, the laws of child placement must be recast both to provide fair warning for parents and children and to restrict the power of state officials.* Legislatures, therefore, should define prospectively and with greater precision than they currently do their responses to the question of primary focus, which is: "What must be established to overcome the strong presumptions in law (a) that parents have the right, the capacity, and the obligation to care for their children in accord with their own notions of child rearing; and (b) that children have

---

* It is another matter to determine whether a particular ground for intervention, even though it satisfies the requisites of fair warning and power restriction, is in the best interests of families and children. See Part Two.

the right to uninterrupted and permanent membership in a family with such parents?"

But specificity of statutory language will never be enough to preclude unjustifiable invasions of family privacy or the unnecessary rupturing of familial bonds. Nor will rules be enough to assure that those who unjustifiably violate family integrity will be held accountable for their abuse of power. Rules are only a first and necessary condition for realizing the goals of fair warning and power restriction. Another necessary condition is that those who are empowered to intrude must understand as well as share the philosophy that underlies a policy of minimum coercive state intervention. A tradition in the administration of child placement laws that is sensitive to the notion of family integrity must be fostered.

Further, we must recognize and work to avoid the consequences of a fantasy too often shared by those who formulate and enact justifications and procedures for intrusion. The fantasy is that only the most competent, most skilled, and most sensitive lawyers, judges, doctors, social workers, foster parents, family helpers, and other personnel will implement the grounds for intrusion under the laws of child placement. There will always be a substantial number in authority who will prevent this fantasy from becoming a realistic expectation. For that reason it is important to place a heavy burden of proof upon those who are empowered to intrude. It is equally important to establish procedures for intrusion which make highly visible the function, nature, and degree of intrusion that is justified at each point of decision.

QUESTIONS FOR DECISION

Guided by the doctrine of minimum state intervention and the requirements of fair warning and power restriction, we can identify and clarify the critical decisions in a child placement process by focusing on three questions:

> 1. *WHAT SHOULD CONSTITUTE* PROBABLE CAUSE *FOR INQUIRY BY AGENTS OF THE STATE INTO INDIVIDUAL PARENT-CHILD RELATIONSHIPS AND WHAT SHOULD THEY BE REQUIRED TO* FIND *BEFORE BEING AUTHORIZED TO SEEK MODIFICATION OR TERMINATION OF A SPECIFIC PARENT-CHILD RELATIONSHIP?*

What events provide reasonable bases for authorizing an investigation by a child protective services agency or by a court in order to determine whether an action should be brought to establish the need to modify or terminate a parent-child relationship? Should, for example, the imprisonment, hospitalization, or death of a parent, the divorce of parents, or a child's poor performance at school be treated as triggering events?

What must an inquiry uncover before parents can be forced to defend their entitlement to care for and represent their child? For example, should "physical neglect," "emotional neglect," spanking for discipline, a parent's continued absence from a child, or a parent's express wish to give up a child be considered sufficient for authorizing an agency to initiate an action and a court to determine who will be the child's caretaker or parent?

Whatever constitutes a ground for modification or termination would, of course, constitute a ground for investigation. However, not all grounds for inquiry would necessarily constitute a sufficient cause for seeking to modify or terminate a relationship. For example, the imprisonment or death of a parent might be justification for an inquiry only to determine whether a child has another parent or whether provision has been made for his care.

Further, even if a ground for modification or termination could be established, there would be no justification for initiating an action if the state knew beforehand that it could not offer a less detrimental alternative.

2. WHAT SHOULD CONSTITUTE SUFFICIENT CAUSE FOR THE STATE TO MODIFY OR TERMINATE A PARENT-CHILD RELATIONSHIP?

How heavy an evidentiary burden must be met before the court is authorized to find that a ground for modifying or terminating a particular parent-child relationship has been established? On whom should the burden of persuasion rest? "This burden is said to have both a location and a weight: the location specifies the party that loses if the burden is not met, and the weight specifies how persuasive the evidence must be in order to carry the burden." [7]

3. IF THERE IS SUFFICIENT CAUSE FOR MODIFICATION OR TERMINATION, WHICH OF THE AVAILABLE ALTERNATIVE PLACEMENTS IS THE LEAST DETRIMENTAL?

The guidelines which we developed in *Beyond the Best Interests of the Child* were designed to pour content into the meaning of "least detrimental available alternative" and thus to enable a court or agency to answer this question. If the state cannot or will not provide something better, even if it did not know this at the time the action was initiated, the least detrimental alternative would be to let the *status quo* persist, however unsatisfactory that might be.[8]

STAGES OF DECISION

The three questions are seldom, if ever, confronted separately in child placement decisions. Yet each question is, in a real sense, answered in a continuous, though often muddled, flow of decisions by legislators, child care agency personnel, and judges. Since the answers and the sequence in which they are reached directly affect and often undermine society's commitment to family integrity, there is a need to refine further and to identify for separate consideration the three critical stages of decision in the law of child placement which correspond to these three questions. They are the stages of *invocation, adjudication,* and *disposition.* Each stage is defined in terms of functions and in terms of the degree and kind of coercive intrusion on family integrity that should be authorized.

Invocation has two functions. One is to determine whether to *investigate* a particular child's condition or circumstances. The other, if the results of the investigation warrant it, is to *commence a legal action* to overcome the presumption of parental autonomy and to obtain a court order authorizing the modification or termination of a familial relationship.

Adjudication has three functions. First, it is to *require the state* to make *full disclosure,* particularly to the parents concerned, of the statutory ground—the facts that constitute a particular justification for intervention—for seeking the authority to modify or terminate. Second, it is to *provide parents with an opportunity to respond* on their own behalf and as representatives of their child to the state's claim. Finally, it is to *determine* whether a *statutory ground* for supervening parental autonomy has been established.

The functions of *disposition* depend upon what is determined at adjudication. If the court adjudicates that no ground has been established, *dismissal of the action* is of course the only function. However, if the court adjudicates that a statutory ground has been established, that the presumption of parental autonomy has been overcome by the state or waived by parents (for example, by those who cannot agree on who shall have custody in a divorce proceeding), the individual child's interest becomes the paramount consideration.* Disposition then has three functions. The first is to *pro-*

---

* Until an adjudication that the presumption of parental autonomy has been overcome, the parents remain qualified to represent the interests of the entire family.

"Of course, the needs of the individual family members do not automatically coincide with each other. Practical steps taken for the benefit of one are often at the same time not in the interest of another. Families vary according to preference being given either to the father's or the mother's or the children's concerns. However, so long as the family is held together by bonds of affection and mutual dependency, whatever arrangements are arrived at pay at least partial regard to all its members." [9]

vide *all parties* to the adjudication with an *opportunity to inform the court* of their respective views about what placement alternatives are available and would best meet the needs of the child. The second is to *recognize the child's status* as a *party* and to assure him of an opportunity for a *conflict-free representation* of his own interests. The third and ultimate function is for the court to *determine the child's placement* and the conditions of this placement. In effect, an *adjudication* which does not lead directly to dismissal becomes a *suspended judgment*. This ought not to be acted upon until the court decides, following a hearing in which the child now has party status, what *disposition* will provide him with the least detrimental placement to accord with his best interests.[10]

DEGREES OF INTRUSION

Coercive intrusion may vary in kind and degree at each decision stage, depending upon the function of the decision and who makes it. When child protective services, for example, invoke the process by making inquiry about a particular child or family, the state intrudes. State agencies further intrude when they initiate an action by charging a ground for intervention. Such intrusions are violations of family privacy. Except in emergencies involving the risk of serious bodily injury to the child, parents should be left free to continue to care for the child and to represent his interests through the adjudication stage until they have been disqualified by proof of the ground charged. Once there is an adjudication that a ground has been established, the state is authorized to intrude further (a) by appointing counsel to represent the child's interest during the disposition phase; and (b) by placing the child in accordance with its notions of his best interests.[11]

In divorce it is the parents who invoke the process. In effect they waive their autonomy by asking the court to make a disposition. The degree of initial intrusion varies with the extent to which the court determines custody against the wishes of at least one of the parents. The state further intrudes if the court is authorized, as it is but ought not to be, to make a disposition which limits the autonomy of the custodial parent through the imposition of conditions and by the retention of continuing jurisdiction.[12] Such invasions of the integrity of the "new" family serve no legitimate function of the disposition stage. They violate the principle of minimum state intervention and in effect create a classification of families which are discriminated against.

The degree of intrusion on family integrity at each stage of decision should be no greater than that which is necessary to fulfill the function of the decision. This is because any interference with family privacy alters the relationships between family members and undermines the effectiveness of parental authority. Therefore we propose that three corollaries of our policy of minimum state intervention become guiding principles in the formulation and administration of the laws of child placement. They are the principles of *least intrusive invocation, least intrusive adjudication,* and *least intrusive disposition.*

Under these principles, for example, intrusion at

invocation would never be justified once the state became aware that it did not have the resources to provide a less detrimental alternative even if it were able to establish a ground for intervention. Further, intrusion at invocation would be kept to the minimum consistent with fact-finding. This principle recognizes that if the evidence is insufficient to adjudicate a ground for supervening parental authority, the case would be dismissed and the child would remain with his parents. On the part of the parents, such investigations may arouse anger toward the child who is the "cause" of the intrusions, and this may be followed by punitive action and increasing family tension. Children, on their part, react even to temporary infringement of parental autonomy with anxiety, diminishing trust, loosening of emotional ties, or an increasing tendency to be out of control. The younger the child, and the greater his own helplessness and dependence, the stronger is his need to experience his parents as his lawgivers—safe, reliable, all-powerful, and independent.

We urge, therefore, that at no stage should intrusion on any family be authorized unless probable and sufficient cause for the coercive action has been established in accord with limits prospectively and precisely defined by the legislature.

With this in mind we focus primarily on the first two points of decision in the child placement process as we seek to determine and define what grounds ought to be sufficient to justify *invocation* or an *adjudication* to modify or terminate a parent-child relationship.

Part Two

Grounds for Intervention

INTRODUCTION

The grounds we propose are intended to replace the existing justifications for coercive state intervention concerning parent-child relationships in abandonment, abuse, adoption, dependency, divorce, foster care, neglect, and separation proceedings.*

In defining these grounds we have sought (a) to satisfy the requisites of fair warning and power restraint; (b) to take into account the standard of the least detrimental alternative; and (c) to abide by our preference for minimum state intrusion on family integrity. Each ground authorizes the state to evaluate, terminate, or otherwise modify the legal relationships between parents and child. The principle of minimum state intervention is meant to apply, from the child's vantage point, to ongoing relationships with his caretakers, who may or may not be his lawful parents at the time a ground is invoked. In a case, for example, involving a child in the longtime care of persons who are not his legal parents, it is the intrusion upon that

---

* We do not address the issues posed by delinquency statutes or by the variously labeled "Person/Child/Minor/Juvenile in Need of Supervision" (PINS, CHINS, MINS, or JINS) statutes. But we do share the view that these so-called status offenses—"[a] juvenile's acts of misbehavior, ungovernability, or unruliness which do not violate the criminal law" [1]—should be abolished as grounds for coercive state intervention.[2] Children should be held by the state to no higher and to no different standards of conduct than those to which the state holds adults.[3] However, the authorized dispositional responses for such prohibited conduct by children should accord with the least detrimental alternative available once any special societal needs for protecting others from danger have been met.[4] Further, we do not review, endorse, or recommend the amendment of grounds for intervention concerned, for example, with the refusal of parents to comply with laws relating to immunization, education, and child labor.[5]

28

relationship which must be minimized. Thus the preference for minimum coercive intervention by the state always applies to a child's *de facto* (ongoing) family, even though, at the time of invocation, it may not be his *de jure* (legal) family.

Chapter 3

Parental Requests for the State to Place the Child

THE REQUEST BY A SEPARATING PARENT FOR THE COURT TO DETERMINE CUSTODY SHOULD BE A GROUND FOR INTERVENTION

Under this ground, intervention is justified only when one or both separating parents, whether married or unmarried, bring to the court their disagreement about the custody of their children. A child is thus (a) *protected from* intrusion if his separating parents can decide to continue to care for him jointly or separately or to entrust his care to a third party; * and (b) *protected by* state intervention if either of his parents requests the court to choose which of them is to be responsible for his custody and care.

Upon adjudication of this ground, the court

---

* Separating parents could choose to leave their custody agreement unrecorded or have it officially recorded to assure that it be recognized for tax or other noncustodial purposes. Joint custody is discussed in the Epilogue in the New Edition of *Beyond the Best Interests of the Child* (New York: Free Press, 1979).

31

would conduct a disposition hearing to determine which parent would provide the least detrimental alternative for the children who are the subject of disagreement. Separating parents may be in agreement about the custody arrangements for some but not all of their children. Under a policy of least intrusive adjudication and disposition the court would be empowered to determine only the custody of those children about whom the parents could not agree.* Further, the court would not have the authority to make a temporary disposition pending its final disposition unless asked to do so by a parent.

By failing to find their own way of resolving their disagreements about custody, separating parents voluntarily give up an important part of their autonomy. By turning to the court, they open up the otherwise "private realm of family life which the state cannot enter." [2] They significantly alter the parent-child relationship; they deprive their child of insulation from direct contact with the law. He is exposed to the impersonal direction and coercion of the court. Since there is little possibility of the child's entering into any intimate relationship with the court, there is also no likelihood that he will identify with the attitudes and

* If possible, courts should avoid separating siblings. Children raised together have a common background and experience that usually is characterized by companionship, rivalry, and mutual support in times of common threat or need. Staying together enables children to support each other by buffering the traumatic family breakup. It provides children with a sense of ongoing community, the continuity that strengthens them in coping with felt threats to future security and self-esteem, and with guilt feelings and associated defensive reactions. [1]

rulings of the new authority over his life. Therefore, the court's discretion at the disposition stage should be limited by the scope of the dispute, and as little time as possible should elapse before the child's position under a personal parental authority is fully restored.*

IMPLICATIONS

Divorce or separation of married parents would no longer be a sufficient ground in and of itself for invocation, adjudication, or disposition.[4] Children of unwed parents would be regarded no differently than the children of married parents who divorce or separate. This ground is designed, in accord with the continuity guideline, to restrain the state from forcing parents who separate to abdicate their role as exclusive representatives of their children. It leaves them free to work out for themselves, if they can, the custody and care arrangements that they believe will best serve the interests of their child and their now divided family.[5]

THE REQUEST BY EITHER OR BOTH PARENTS FOR THE COURT TO TERMINATE THEIR RIGHTS IN A CHILD SHOULD BE A GROUND FOR INTERVENTION

This ground is designed to provide parents with a relatively stigma-free and nonviolent opportunity to in-

---

* Courts would lack jurisdiction to entertain a noncustodial parent's petition to change custody, whether ordered by the court or voluntarily arranged and recorded by the separating parents, unless, as with any family, the petition alleged one of the grounds for intervention. A "change of circumstances" is not one of the grounds for intervention that we propose.[3]

voke the child placement process. Its purpose is to maximize every unwanted child's chances of being placed in a family that wants him. Once parents decide that they wish to have their rights terminated, the child by definition becomes unwanted. That some parents might want to give up responsibility for their child runs counter to society's wishful thinking that a parent's love is one factor which will endure. This belief makes it difficult to give recognition to the real facts.[6] To deny that many pregnancies and children are unwanted would be to ignore—to the detriment of both child and parents—clear and unmistakable signals that a child's well-being, psychological * and physical, may be in jeopardy.

This ground permits parents who do not wish to raise their child or who do not want or cannot afford the abortion of an unwanted pregnancy to arrange for the child's care without first being "forced" to place him at risk. No matter how difficult or easy it may be for parents to give up a child, this ground respects the wishes of the parents of an unwanted child and provides them with an opportunity to act responsibly. This ground does not invite the state to be judgmental. Parents are not required to satisfy an agency or a court that their decision to terminate is for "good cause." [7] They, as adults, are left to determine their own "good cause"—to deal with their own motivations.

This ground is intended to provide only for the relinquishment of unwanted children, not of children

* This ground identifies a set of circumstances that may be covered under current law by "emotional neglect," a phrase that is too broad and vague to meet our requisites of a ground for intervention. See Chapter 5.

who are really wanted. The court should determine
whether the state (a) had coerced or deceived petitioning parents into surrendering their child, or (b) had
failed to offer available supportive services which might
make it possible for them and their child to remain together. Such an inquiry is not intended to place pressure
on the parents to keep their children. Therefore, the
court could not require petitioning parents to justify
their decision to relinquish their child. Rather, the
court's function is to find out whether the state can
relieve them of any demands which led them to petition for termination. It is to assure that their decisions
are voluntary.[8] This ground rests on the presumption
that forcing parents to keep an unwanted child not only
impinges upon their autonomy but also provides a most
detrimental placement.

IMPLICATIONS

This ground provides an open and nonjudgmental process for parents to give up their unwanted children without first having to "abandon," "abuse," or
"neglect" them.[9] It acknowledges a right which exists
but which when exercised is often met with disapproval,
except possibly in the case of unwed and minor parents.
This ground should relegate "the Dickensian portrait of
mothers driven to leave babes in doorways . . . to the
dark recesses of the past." [10] It should reduce the fre-
quency of such cases as that of the agency which refused
to abide by a mother's request that her son be placed in
adoption. After being told by a social worker that she
must reconsider her request, the mother returned home,
assaulted her son, and brought him battered to the

worker, saying, "I really meant it. You'll believe me now. I want him adopted." [11] In the language of the economist, this ground would enable parents to rectify their mistake "at lower cost—to them, and to the child —than if they were forced to retain custody of the child until their neglect reached the point when the state would intervene. . . ." [12]

The parental decision to give up a child means that the child is unwanted. The interests of parent and child coincide when the parent voluntarily relinquishes him. Legal termination of the relationship would thus comport with the parents' wishes and provide the child with an opportunity to become a member of a family where he will be wanted and where his emotional and physical needs will be met.

This ground is not an easy way out or an undeserved reward for an "unwanting" parent. It provides an opportunity to protect some children from avoidable risks. It is a means of seeking to meet a child's need to be wanted, to love and be loved. While the unwanting parent will also profit from the granting of a petition to terminate, it is the welfare of the child which remains the paramount value to be protected.* [13]

---

* Adoption offers to such children the best possible second chance to form the permanent relationships which are vital for their development. Nevertheless, it would be a mistake to assume that the fact of having been unwanted remains without repercussions. Whether entry into the new family happens soon after birth or somewhat later, children use the information about their adopted state in a variety of ways. They may develop ideas about their own unworthiness which made the "real" parents give them away. They may fear that, for the same reason, abandonment will be repeated. On the other hand, they may deny their resentment about the re-

jection and imagine that they have been "stolen," i.e., kidnapped against the parents' will. For the same reason, they may idealize the biological parents in their fantasies and use this as a weapon against the adoptive parents on occasions when children normally feel angry, frustrated, or otherwise in revolt against parental authority.[14]

Chapter 4

Familial Bonds Between Children and Longtime Caretakers Who Are Not Their Parents

THE REQUEST BY A CHILD'S LONGTIME CARETAKERS TO BECOME HIS PARENTS OR THE REFUSAL BY LONGTIME CARETAKERS TO RELINQUISH HIM TO HIS PARENTS OR TO A STATE AGENCY SHOULD BE A GROUND FOR INTERVENTION

This ground is designed to reduce the number of so-called "temporary" placements and to promote continuity of care by encouraging the use of supportive services within a family. At the same time, it is meant to safeguard the familial bonds that do develop between children placed outside their homes and the longtime caretakers who want to be their legally designated parents. This ground is intended to prevent child care agencies and long-absent parents, natural or adoptive, from keeping their children in limbo or from forcing them to separate from psychologically real parents who wish to continue to care for them.

This ground rests upon our understanding that every child requires continuity of care, an unbroken relationship with at least one adult who is and wants to be directly responsible for his daily needs. It recognizes the importance of the psychological ties that develop over time between a child and the adults who continuously provide for his day-to-day care. It acknowledges that the existence of these familial bonds need not depend upon the technicality of the biological or legal relationship between a child and an adult. Where longtime foster parents, for example, return a child's affection and make him feel wanted, "looked after," and appreciated, crucial bonds usually form between them which cannot be disturbed without harm.[1]

This ground recognizes, in terms of a child's sense of time, the significance of both the length of separation from parents and the duration of care by substitute parents. It is founded on our knowledge that no child can be put on ice indefinitely—until absent parents are able and wish to recover him—without putting his health and well-being in jeopardy.* From a child's point of view, no absence from his parents is temporary

* The lack of common sense about this is vividly reflected in the attitude of a young unmarried mother who wished to place her newborn son in longtime foster care. Insisting that she would not sign the child away for adoption, she said, "By the time he is ready to go to school, he can live with me. He would, then, be *company.*"

if it exceeds the period of time during which the child, always according to his age and stage of development, can preserve inner ties to them. Nor are new care arrangements temporary if they extend to a time when the new relationships occupy more and more the place of former ones or, for infants placed at birth, become the primary ones. The very young infant, for example, may not yet have formed an attachment, but—out of his acute sense of helplessness—will develop one rather rapidly with his new caretakers. For the older child, the quality of his psychological tie to his absent parents will determine his capacity to sustain a separation from them before he acquires a new "psychological parent." Once new psychological relationships form, separation from the substitute parents becomes no less painful and no less damaging to a child than his separation from natural or adoptive caretaking parents.*

The motivations of adult caretakers for accepting a child who is not their own will affect the speed with which their feelings develop for him.[2] Their acceptance of the child may happen much less rapidly than the child's acceptance of them. Or they may accept the child long before he himself has let go of the tie to his own parents. Under this ground the time for intervention is when both child and caretaker have turned to and accepted one another. At that time, when the child has

* Indeed, to the extent that such separations are repeated, as in multiple foster care placements, they make each subsequent opportunity for attachment less promising and less trustworthy than the initial or prior one. Each subsequent separation leaves the child more vulnerable and less able to develop and sustain the previous level of attachment—resting merely on "stomach" love rather than real love.

a psychological parent and his caretakers have a "psychological child," [3] the rights of the "absent" parents should be terminated in favor of the "new" familial ties. These bonds deserve the same protection that ongoing relationships between children and their natural or adoptive parents deserve and traditionally receive.

Though the complex process of forming psychological parent-child relationships is not beyond description, its timetable cannot be set precisely. Yet, given the present state of knowledge and the limitations of law, we have come to conclude that specific statutory periods, when coupled with the explicit wish of the longtime caretaker to become permanently responsible for a child's care, are the most reliable indicators and the least detrimental means that we have for giving the "new" relationships full legal recognition. In setting specific time spans, we purposely credited prior ties with greater longevity than they would normally require. We chose greater-than-normal lengths of time that a child would have to be in the continuous custody of the same caretakers before these ties had either shifted to them or started to take significant root.

We did not come easily to the conclusion that longtime caretakers could be defined in terms of specific statutory periods. In *Beyond the Best Interests of the Child* we said: "The process through which a new child-parent status emerges is too complex and subject to too many individual variations for the law to provide a rigid statutory timetable." [4] Even when conservatively graded according to a child's age at the time of placement, such periods are arbitrary and open to exception. In work sessions on this book we initially argued that in contested cases between longtime caretakers and natural or adoptive parents a child's fate should not be decided on such objective data alone, but that corroboration from subjective findings about his relationship to them should be required.* We were satisfied, however, that the express wish of longtime caretakers to continue their care on a permanent basis was sufficient to imply that they were prepared to make the commitment to him as a "wanted" child.[5] On the other hand, the words of children, their overt attitudes, and even their allegiances are often too fickle for experts to evaluate correctly. To arrive at a trustworthy opinion of a particular child's true mental state as to who are his psychological parents is a matter which taxes the skills of even the most experienced clinicians—skills not easily taught and usually beyond the training of courts, social service personnel, and other mental health professionals. Such opinions are often not obtainable at all. More than that, the many necessarily intrusive sessions with a child that a clinician requires before rendering an opinion would create intolerable periods of uncertainty. And that opinion would seldom do more than confirm what the passage of time implies.

Given the current state of knowledge and of clinical know-how, there is in the child placement process only one procedure for ascertaining with certainty who a child's psychological parents are and what remnants of affection, if any, are left to connect him with

---

* These concerns do not go to cases in which there is not, following the passage of the statutory period, a wanting natural or adoptive parent ready and willing to resume full-time care and custody of the child.

absent biological or adoptive parents. That procedure is to test over time the child's reactions to attempted reunions. Through deterioration of sleep, of control of aggression, of attention span, and of school performance, children show that they feel threatened at the very core of their personalities by the thought of reunion with their estranged parents.[6] These signs represent uncontrovertible evidence which can only be ignored at the child's peril. But the incremental assurance which such court-sponsored human experiments give judges and social workers about whose claim to recognize is won at a price too high for the child. These trial periods disrupt the child's existing life situation and shake his security and trust in the protective powers of his long-time caretakers to whom he should be returned whenever the experiment "fails." *

We conclude therefore that the disruption of developmental processes which might otherwise carry the child forward toward normal adulthood is a risk that no child should be forced to take. Such tests con-

---

* For this reason, hearings concerned with terminating the relationship between foster children and their longtime caretakers must take place before separating them, not after. "An erroneous wrenching of the nurturing bonds between the long term foster child and his long term foster family is the kind of damage that is not fully — or even substantially — recompensable even by ordering a resumption of the broken relationships. In terms of irreparable injury, an erroneous breaking up of delicate and complex long term foster family relationships is far more serious than would be such an unthinkable action as, for example, an agency intentionally breaking a child's arm for some therapeutic purpose, recognizing that such a mistake may be 'corrected' by resetting the limb which, though scarred, may grow together again as 'strong' as it ever was."[7]

stitute gross violations of the principles of least intrusive invocation and adjudication and jeopardize the child's chances for a satisfactory disposition.[8] Unless and until better, quicker, and safer methods have been found to determine the state of a young child's vital emotional ties, this ground for terminating old, and at the same time for giving legal recognition to "new," parental rights must rest on objective data which are readily obtainable with a minimum of intrusion.

Beyond satisfying the requisites of fair warning and power restraint, the specific time spans that we now propose for defining "longtime caretaker" thus take into account a number of factors. They are sensitive to the societal preference for maintaining natural and adoptive parent-child relationships. They are sensitive to the painful harm done to children by forcibly separating them from their no longer "temporary" caretakers in trial-and-error efforts to restore legal relationships that are almost certainly no longer tenable human relationships. They recognize the limits of knowledge—that there is no litmus paper for testing when a substitute parent has become a particular child's psychological parent. They are conservatively set in terms of a child's sense of time and the different consequences that disruptions of continuity have for children of different ages.* They become operative only if the ongoing care-

* The younger a child, the weaker are his emotional resources for managing a "long" separation from his parents and the more likely it is that significant psychological ties will have developed between him and his caretakers. Consequently, the younger the child at the time he is placed with his longtime caretaker, the more damaging is the severance of the familial bonds between them. Children who have suffered multiple foster placements may

takers make it clear that they are willing to assume full responsibility for the child.

We propose the following statutory periods during which a child is in the direct and continuous care of the same adult(s) as maximum intervals beyond which it would be unreasonable to presume that a child's residual ties with his absent parents are more significant than those that have developed between him and his longtime caretakers:

(a) 12 months for a child up to the age of 3 years at the time of placement;

(b) 24 months for a child from the age of 3 years at the time of placement.

With one exception, these time spans coupled with the longtime caretaker's wish to continue custody are reliable indicators for granting legal recognition to the "new" relationships and for terminating the legal relationship between the children, absent parents, and state agencies.* [10]

---

make superficial attachments but are unwilling or unable to make deep primary ones.[9]

* We recognize, as did Mr. Justice Douglas in a 1974 United States Supreme Court opinion considering the adequacy of a statutory definition of "family" for zoning purposes, that "every line drawn by a legislature leaves some out that might well have been included." He added:

"Mr. Justice Holmes made the point a half century ago.

"'When a legal distinction is determined, as no one doubts that it may be, between night and day, childhood and maturity, or any other extremes, a point has to be fixed or a line has to be drawn, or gradually picked out by successive decisions, to mark where the change takes place. Looked at by itself without regard to the necessity behind it the line or point seems arbitrary. It might

For some children in the older age group, the statutory period of 24 months or more, no matter how strong the wish of the longtime caretakers to keep "their" child, may not be a sufficient basis for terminating the legal relationships to absent parents who wish to regain custody. Some older children may hold emotional attachments to absent parents all the more fiercely and possessively the longer the separation lasts. Their early, long-standing, psychological ties, even though not assisted by current experience, may interfere with the formation of new psychological attachments to the fostering adults no matter how genuine their affection may be or how real the satisfactions they offer.[12] In such instances, the absent parents will have remained the psychological ones in spite of their absence, and a return to them (however painful to the longtime caretakers) will be welcomed by the child and will provide him with the least detrimental alternative. To protect such children and their legal parents from unjustified dispositions, this ground provides a special hearing for any child over 5 years of age,

> (a) who, at the time of placement, had been in the continuous care of his parents for not less than the 3 preceding years; *and*
> (b) who had *not* been separated from his parents because they inflicted or attempted to inflict serious bodily injury upon him or

---

as well or nearly as well be a little more to one side or the other. But when it is seen that a line or point there must be, and that there is no mathematical or logical way of fixing it precisely, the decision of the legislature must be accepted unless we can say that it is very wide of any reasonable mark.' " [11]

were convicted of a sexual offense against him.*

Drawing upon the best available professional personnel, and recognizing the limits of such inquiries, the hearing would be designed to determine whether the child's absent parents are still his psychological parents and whether his return to them would be the least detrimental alternative.† In the event that such evidence is inconclusive, the child's relationship to his longtime caretakers should be given legal recognition.

In all other cases, the critical factor in defining the longtime caretakers and for determining a child's entitlement to remain with them is the length of time that a child is in their continuous custody, not the period of time that he is separated from his absent parents. The statutory periods are time *with,* not time *away from.*[14] These periods would control the disposition decision except in cases involving the group of older children whom we have identified for special attention. Following adjudication in which this ground is established, parental rights would be terminated and the longtime caretakers would be recognized as the child's legal parents.

The child would be entitled to permanent membership in the substitute family. Adoption is preferable.

---

* These gross failures of care are discussed as grounds for intervention in Chapter 5.

† Experts should clarify for themselves the distinction between their roles as investigators and therapists. They must make clear to those they examine that, as experts responding to agency and court requests, their relationship to those they interview and observe is neither confidential nor necessarily benign.[13]

But when longtime caretakers who want to continue the relationship do not wish to adopt, it would generally be less detrimental for the child to continue in that relationship than to break it. He must not be made the victim of a state policy which favors adoption for adoption's sake. Nonadoptive but permanent relationships should be given recognition as *care with tenure*. Such children would be insulated from intrusion by state agencies and former parents. They could expect the continuity of care and family membership usually associated with adoption.

In foster placement *without* tenure, the shared authority between the fostering adults and the child care agency is by no means a matter of indifference to the children, who realize the insecurity of their position. There is a wide gap between the secure way in which a child can feel settled in his own family with fully autonomous biological or adoptive parents and the insecurity caused by the constant need to find a balance between the competing demands of fostering parents and external authorities. This insecurity produces in some children a forced obedience to avoid being "sent away," while in others it often leads to revolt in order to test the limits of acceptance. In any case, it delays or prevents for the older child the acquisition of new psychological parents, great as is his need for them. Legal recognition of care with tenure could help meet that need.

This ground and the dispositional guides must include provision for discouraging agencies from pursuing a policy of multiple placements. Such a malignant policy is particularly unacceptable as a technique for preserving the rights of absent parents who are not prepared to resume responsibility for the regular and continuous care of their child. Therefore, if the foster parents want the child, and even if the statutory period for them to qualify as longtime caretakers has not elapsed, a child care agency can remove him only to return him permanently to his legal parents, not to place him elsewhere.*

The specific time periods for each age category provide the least intrusive modes of invocation and adjudication for establishing psychological parent-child relationships. In addition, they give advance warning to parents and state agencies of the consequences that will follow long separations, however well intentioned. Without discouraging essential temporary placements, this ground is meant to force a realistic evaluation of

---

* There is a need for a truly temporary form of foster care. A decision to place a child in such care must carry with it an expectation for all parties, including the court, that the child will shortly—in accord with the child's sense of time—be restored to his family, and that during the period of separation provision can be made for keeping alive the ties that bond child and absent parents. Disturbances to the continuity of his ties with parental figures and of their ties to him must be kept to an absolute minimum. Their reunion must be the *goal* of foster care. What this will mean both in terms of provisions for maintaining reciprocity of affectionate relationships will depend in large measure on the child's age at the time he is placed in foster care and upon the extent and form of accessibility of child and parents to each other during the period of separation. The younger the child, the shorter should be the duration of such a placement if it is to be temporary. Temporary foster parents have the double task of supplying for the child the missing parental care without at the same time alienating the child's feelings for the absent parents. This is a delicate and extremely difficult job.[15]

both the circumstances which prompt voluntary and involuntary separations and the likelihood that the ties between child and absent parents can be kept alive. For example, recognition that the circumstances that force parents and child to separate are chronic and that the probability of long separation is high should cause an increased use of supportive resources to keep families together. But when "temporary" placements become long-term, for whatever reason, the familial bonds that develop between the child and his caretakers must not be shattered by state action on behalf of absent parents or because of agency policies.*

No matter who invokes this ground, the continuity guideline dictates that the child remain in the custody of his caretaker until final disposition.[16] Moreover, the child's-sense-of-time guideline requires that disposition, including all appeals, be resolved as a matter of urgency within the shortest period possible.[17]

IMPLICATIONS

The *Appleton* case [18] provides an example of the harm that this ground is meant to prevent. The Juvenile

---

* If the circumstances, including provisions for preserving existing ties, justify foster care, the court should establish a date in advance, not to exceed the appropriate statutory period beyond which that arrangement would no longer be temporary. Each case should be tagged to resurface for review shortly before the expiration of that maximum. Such an *early warning* system would uncover those cases in which the child had not yet been restored to his family and allow time to consider the possibility of permanent restoration with or without supportive services. If that is found not to be a reasonable option, it would allow the child's relationship with his caretakers to be made permanent even before the statutory period is reached.

Court judge inauspiciously began his opinion in that case with these words:

> Among the few unpleasant burdens which fall upon a Trial Judge is the responsibility to determine the fate of a young child.

The Appletons were foster parents of Tom, a 5-year-old who had lived with them for the last 4 years of his life. They had asked the court not to return Tom to his biological parents as demanded by the County Child Care Service, but rather to allow him to remain in their custody and, if possible, to be adopted by them. The court declared that the county agency had "real custody" of Tom and the authority to determine what was best for him. Yet it acknowledged that: "If . . . the best interests of the child received paramount consideration, this court could readily determine that young Tom would obtain greater advantages and benefits" with the Appletons. They were psychological parents for Tom. From his point of view, not the law's, they were his only parents. Nevertheless, the judge observed:

> [T]he agency to whom the child was awarded . . . is satisfied that the causes which gave rise to the committal no longer exist and the child should be brought back to its natural parents. . . . The Appletons accepted the child with knowledge of the terms of the agreement and received money compensation for their services. The agreement also provided that the Appletons were not to institute any proceedings with a view

to adoption or placement. While a child's custody should not rest alone upon a contract and a child regarded as mere chattel, the natural parents have natural rights and obligations and are entitled to their child.

Finally, in an apparent effort to reinforce its decision, the court ritualistically recited:

Under the present Juvenile Court Act . . . it is expressly stated that the unity of the family whenever possible is to be preserved. *The family itself is an institution whose sanctity must be preserved* [emphasis supplied].

The court could not recognize that the institution to "be preserved" was a living human one, not a fictitious legal one. It could not restrain the state from separating Tom from his real—his psychological—parents. The integrity and stability of Tom's family was thus shattered by court order.

Unintended separations of children from their parents happen only too frequently in war, or in peacetime, due to air, train, or traffic accidents. In all such instances, the deprived child can be certain of the sympathy of a public which realizes that something major and irreparable has occurred that disrupts his life, shakes his security, and impairs his chances to develop into a healthy, well-functioning adult. To be orphaned without preparation, to be forced to dismantle existing emotional ties and fashion new ones with hitherto unknown people, is no easy task for any human being. Children are especially unequipped for such losses.

For the child who is the innocent victim of such traumatic happenings, whether brought about by accident or by a judge's decision, the vanished parents are beyond reach. To Tom, it makes little difference whether his psychological parents are natural or longtime caretakers with little or no legal claim. Nor does it make any difference to him if the unknown adults to whom he is reassigned are in fact his biological parents. Whenever biological parents succeed in reclaiming a child after years of estrangement—after years in a substitute family—the child's feelings of being wanted and secure are jeopardized. Equally threatened are many developmental advances which are firmly rooted in the reciprocal interchange of affection between an immature dependent being and his familiar adult caretakers.

Instead of protecting the development and emotional well-being of the child, the *Appleton* court chose to safeguard child care agency policy, to enforce a contract, and to respect a legal, not an actual, relationship. Even if a contract theory deserves recognition, there is no reason why the child must be sacrificed to the injured party. In any other breach of contract case involving personal service the court can award no more than money damages. When adults are concerned, it cannot require specific performance of personal services, as the Appleton Court did when it ordered Tom to leave his home to live with people who, from his point of view, were strangers.*

* Courts must begin to distinguish between finding a violation of parental rights and fashioning a remedy for that violation.[19]

Finally, as if unaware of the consequences of his decision, the judge pronounced another principle of minimum state intervention and continuity in support of a ruling which violently defied it:

> The state is and should be restrained in removing a child from its parents except under the most unusual conditions.

And so it should be. But because the judge mechanistically traced blood ties to identify Tom's family and parents, he was unable to apply his own guidelines. He could not or would not recognize which of the two competing units was Tom's real family and who among the competing adults were Tom's parents. He ignored 4 years of affectionate care. Had the "longtime caretaker" ground for intervention been part of the child placement code, the court could not have authorized the state to intrude so massively upon Tom's ongoing relationships and to shatter for him and his longtime caretakers their real family.

These concerns about Tom's well-being proved to be more than speculative. The events that followed his forced separation illustrate the harm youngsters such as Tom suffer when courts make them the subject of "experiments" designed to reawaken parent-child relationships. About a year after his return "home," Tom's natural father was charged with abusing him. Pending a determination, Tom was forced to enter an orphanage. He remained there for another 5 months until the court ordered him returned to the Appletons.

It relied upon the following report from a child psychiatrist engaged by Tom's court-appointed counsel:

> "Tom is a 6 year old boy [who] is presently showing signs and symptoms of anxiety, nightmares, [and] sleeping difficulties due to the recent confusion, and significant separations. . . .
>
> "When returned to his natural parents over a year ago, there appeared to be an initial adjustment to them. . . . I would describe [it as] a move of helpless surrender to what appeared to be a situation beyond his control. . . . Mr. Appleton is the man he wants to be like, and Mrs. Appleton is the mother whom he feels comforts him and whom he feels he needs so he would not have to hide under the covers with fear at night.
>
> "If Tom remained at the home of his natural parents with his identifications being at the Appletons, I believe there would have been a further worsening of the behavior problems. . . . The uncertainties in this boy's life in the orphanage placement are wearing away at [his] adaptive abilities. Consistency and permanent placement in the boy's psychological home is needed for continued adequate growth and maturation. . . ."

Nine months after Tom's return to the Appletons, they again had to fight to preserve Tom's right to stay. This time the court entertained an action by the natural mother to force Tom to visit her. In order to test the possibility of reestablishing their relationship, the court was willing to put Tom's development at further risk.

Even if his biological parents were ideal, even if they were in all ways superior to the Appletons, and even if the state were in error in its initial decision to place Tom in foster care or to leave him there for more than a temporary period, Tom should never have been used to remedy those mistakes or as an award for damages.* What was once intended to be a "temporary" placement had become permanent. The relationship between Tom and the Appletons deserved recognition and should have been treated with the same finality as the traditional placement of a child with his biological parents. Only in that way could the court have given credibility to its announced policy to favor family unity and judicial "restraint in removing a child from its parents except under the most unusual conditions."

---

* Though they are not and indeed ought not to be relevant to the decision in this case, the unusual facts of Tom's repossession by his biological parents add to the tragedy of the court's action. The record revealed that the biological mother had been responsible for the death of a 1-month-old infant son who suffered a brain hemorrhage after she struck him on the head in anger, that she broke another son's leg in an outburst of temper and later severely burned the same child as punishment, and that she severely kicked a third 16-month-old child in an angry rage. She had been under medical care most of her adult life, including a 2-year commitment to a mental hospital. The biological father had a drinking problem.

Chapter 5

Gross Failures of Parental Care

*THE DEATH OR DISAPPEARANCE OF BOTH
PARENTS, THE ONLY PARENT OR THE
CUSTODIAL PARENT—WHEN COUPLED
WITH THEIR FAILURE TO MAKE
PROVISION FOR THEIR CHILD'S
CUSTODY AND CARE—SHOULD
BE A GROUND FOR
INTERVENTION*

This ground for intervention is designed to provide the state with the authority to discover and to safeguard children for whom no day-to-day care arrangements have been made by parents who die, disappear, are imprisoned or hospitalized. In addition to jeopardizing a child's physical well-being, events of this kind deprive the child emotionally, as do all separations, and also deprive him of representation before the law and within the adult community. An adjudication requires a disposition that will make up for these losses to the extent possible and provide the child with emotional and social as well as physical security.

IMPLICATIONS

Unlike traditional statutes, this ground for intervention does not require establishing the intent of parents to abandon their children. It focuses on the actual plight of the individual child, without regard to parental purpose.[1] At the same time, it acknowledges that parental autonomy includes the right of parents to delegate to others (including relatives, friends, and school personnel who are responsible to them) the custody and care of their children. Imprisonment, hospitalization of parents, or their draft into the armed services, for example, might justify an inquiry as to whether they have made arrangements for the custody and care of their child, and if not, whether an emergency placement is required pending an adjudication. But the death, disappearance, or institutionalization of a parent, in and of itself, justifies no more than an inquiry. It does not justify further intrusion *unless* the parents have not provided for their child's care. This ground rests on the common sense which underlies, for example, a Florida statute that requires honoring the appointment of a child's guardian under his parents' will. As one court interpreted that provision:

No person is in a position to know as well [as the parent] who should have the custody of children. . . . He has observed them throughout their lives. By daily contact he knows their tem-

peraments and habits, and by observation he
knows those who have evidenced the greatest
interest in his children, and those whose moral
and spiritual values are in his judgment conducive to the best interests of his children. A
judge treads on sacred ground when he overrides
the directions of the deceased with reference to
the custody of his children.[2]

Furthermore, this ground codifies the reading given to
the phrase "uncared for" by Judge Rubinow in *Welfare
Commissioner* v. *Anonymous*.[3] In that case, solely on
the basis of a mother's imprisonment, the commissioner
charged that her children were "uncared for" and
should be declared wards of the state. Before her imprisonment, the mother placed these children in the
care of their grandaunt. Making obvious what apparently was not obvious—at least to the commissioner—
Judge Rubinow observed:

[I]f a child is being properly cared for by, for
example, a close relative at the request of a biological parent, the commissioner's construction
would require the court to say that a child is
"uncared for" when, in fact, the child is "cared
for." . . . [T]he commissioner's construction
would have the undesirable consequence of discouraging biological parents from even temporarily entrusting their children to someone
who would give them better care, for, under the
commissioner's construction, even temporarily
entrusting children to a nonbiological parent to

enable the children to be better cared for would make the children "uncared for" and subject to commitment to the commissioner.[4]

Of course, arrangements for temporary care made by absent parents themselves or by the state following an adjudication may become longtime. Such caretakers, on the basis of the ground set forth in Chapter 4, could then make their relationship with the child permanent. But in this case, under the principle of the least intrusive invocation, the mother's imprisonment justified only inquiry as to whether she had made provision for the care of her children.[5]

CONVICTION, OR ACQUITTAL BY REASON OF INSANITY, OF A SEXUAL OFFENSE AGAINST ONE'S CHILD SHOULD BE A GROUND FOR INTERVENTION

This ground for intervention is concerned with the emotional harm caused to children whose parents use them as sexual partners. It applies primarily to the seduced child, not to children who suffer physical harm at the hands of sexually assaulting parents. Like any child whose parent assaults his body, a child who is brutally attacked sexually by his parent experiences shock, pain, and fear as immediate reactions and insecurity, distrust, and dread of repetition as the aftereffects. Such children are covered by the ground (proposed later) that mandates intervention whenever parents, whatever their motivation, inflict serious bodily injury upon their children.

This ground recognizes that the sexual wishes, fantasies, desires, and practices of an immature child are as different from those of an adult as are his bones, physical capacities, and intellectual achievements. The pattern of a child's development toward mature sex is thrown into confusion by any seducing adult who uses the child to satisfy his sexual appetite. Intercourse with children prematurely arouses their genital responses and intimately related erotic feelings.* Such children are overwhelmed emotionally and physically. Though their turmoil may not become immediately visible, the detrimental consequences usually become manifest in adolescent and adult life in the form of unsatisfying personal and sexual relationships. When the seducing adult is actually the child's parent, the damage done to his emotional life is likely to be most severe.[7]

Children are not always unwilling partners in sexual activities initiated by the parent. On the contrary, parental sexual advances are met only too frequently by a child's willingness to cooperate. Initial shock and surprise do not preclude pleasurable erotic excitement from the fulfillment of secret fantasies. Parents are, after all, the first loved people in a child's life toward whom he turns for satisfaction. Indeed, children regularly develop fantasies to become the partner of the parent of the opposite sex and replace the marital partner.[8] Normal as these fantasies are, the child's

* The premature arousal of sexual zones leaves the child with an urge for repeated direct sensual gratification. A seduced child often becomes either a seducer or, as a result of guilt feelings, an inhibited person who is unlikely to enjoy normal sexual activity in later life.[6]

mental health and emotional development depend upon their not being realized. Parents must not allow a child's emotional ties to them to go beyond the limits of affection.

Sexual relations between parent and child tend to remain well-guarded family secrets. When suspicion is aroused, the harm done by inquiry may be more than that caused by not intruding. The harm already inflicted upon the child—and it may be difficult to learn its extent—is aggravated by violations of family integrity, particularly by the investigation that is triggered.[9] Further, since no consensus exists about the proper treatment or about what disposition would be less harmful, there is no justification from the child's point of view for dragging the matter into the open by invoking the child placement process.* For these reasons, justification for separating the child and offending parent seems best left to the criminal law—to its high standard of evidentiary proof and its goal of reinforcing society's moral position. After a conviction or an insanity acquittal, there is no longer any reason for not incurring the risks of disposition, of determining the least detrimental alternative.†

---

* "Treatment" in childhood cannot put the prematurely stimulated sexual appetite to sleep again; at best it may help the child deal with immediate psychological aftereffects. Treatment at a later age deals with pathological consequences—either inhibition or promiscuity.

† This ground's recognition of the limits of law and knowledge about treatment should not obscure our belief that it is desirable for such parents on their own initiative to seek psychological assistance for themselves and their child. The state should provide such opportunities for those who want help.

This ground is therefore limited to children whose parents are convicted, or acquitted by reason of insanity, of a sexual offense against them.[10] It acknowledges that we know enough to declare that a child is harmed even by a parent's nonviolent sexual abuse, but not enough to know that state intervention can offer something less detrimental. Thus, the authority to assume the risks of intervention, including the termination of parental rights, arises only after the parent-child relationship has been severed by the criminal process.

IMPLICATIONS

The American Bar Association Commission on Juvenile Justice Standards has proposed that "[Coercive intervention should be authorized when] a child has been sexually abused by his/her parent or a member of his/her household" (or alternatively, with the addition of "and is seriously harmed physically or emotionally thereby").[11] Such proposals do not satisfy the requisite of fair warning and power restraint. In fact, the Bar Association Commission, aware of many of our concerns, acknowledges that its "standard does not define 'sexual abuse.' "[12] Strangely, it suggests that intervention be authorized not only where the subject action would be a violation of the relevant state penal law but also if it "would have been a violation if the laws are repealed." It underscores an additional reason for our restriction on intervention: "As a factual matter, it may be difficult to distinguish between appropriate displays of affection and fondling or other behavior possibly disturbing or damaging to the child. Although relying on penal laws may, in some cases, result in definitional vagueness, it should suffice since only the most severe types of behavior are ordinarily reported." [13]

The ground we propose, unlike that of the Bar Association, is concerned only with sexual offenses by parents against their children. As their child's representatives, parents are relied upon to meet and manage any problems stemming from their children's sexual relations with each other, with other members of the household, and indeed with outsiders. Our ground would preclude damaging invocation and adjudication proceedings such as those prompted by New York City's Bureau of Child Welfare and condemned by Family Court Judge Dembitz in the case of the Vulon children—Maurice, age 13, Marie, 10, and Michelle, 8.[14] After asking how this "well-spoken, well-dressed, well-groomed, and apparently well-cared for" family became involved with the City's Bureau, Judge Dembitz wrote:

> The Bureau's petition alleges that the three children are left alone and unattended from 3:30 to 5:30 P.M. on week-days; that after Michelle was admitted to Lincoln Hospital "with severe injury to the vaginal area * * * the hospital reported Michelle as an abused child whose injuries were most likely the result of rape, and the circumstances surrounding this incident were unexplained by the parents." The undisputed evidence shows that these allegations are misleading in significant respects.
>
> Both Mr. and Mrs. Vulon work to support the family, Mrs. Vulon as an IBM key punch

operator. She arrives home from work at 5:30 or a few minutes before. The three children generally return from school between 3:30 and 4:30 and then stay in the apartment doing homework. It is questionable whether it would constitute "neglect" to leave habitually well-behaved children of ages 13, 10 and 8, unattended in an apparently secure apartment in the afternoon for the two hours alleged in the petition; possibly self-responsibility to this limited extent, in a family where parents show an over-all affection and concern, may not only be harmless but beneficial. In any event, Mrs. Vulon testified without contradiction that since the troubling incident here involved she had secured someone to stay in the apartment in the afternoons until she returns from work. . . .

The evidence showed that on the afternoon of the incident in issue—which was a partial school holiday—Maurice was in and out of the home doing errands, Marie was washing dishes, and Michelle was first using the vacuum cleaner and then taking a bath. Marie heard Michelle exclaim from the bathroom and saw she was bleeding. Mrs. Vulon came home shortly thereafter, and although the bleeding was not extreme took Michelle to Prospect Hospital. There, because no physician was available, she was referred to Lincoln Hospital. By the time of her arrival at Lincoln the bleeding was more profuse and a physician recommended a surgical procedure under anesthesia for remedial and exploratory purposes. One source of suspicion against the family appears to have been that Mrs. Vulon did not immediately consent to surgery for her daughter; she testified that she had wanted to wait for her husband to arrive from Prospect Hospital, where he had expected to meet them. (Mrs. Vulon, who emigrated from Haiti in 1958, speaks poor English). The father arrived shortly; consent was given forthwith; and the child's condition was soon remedied.

The Lincoln Hospital physician called by petitioner testified that the bleeding was attributable to a laceration of the vagina of about an inch; that he could not estimate the source of the laceration with any certainty except that rape probably was *not* the cause; that the condition was probably due to "trauma" of some other type and could have been self-inflicted.

The erroneous suspicion of rape—which persisted apparently because of a failure to consult this knowledgeable physician—underlay petitioner's allegation as to the parents' failure to explain the circumstances of Michelle's bleeding. Mrs. Vulon did explain the circumstances to petitioner and other interrogators to the extent she could ascertain them from the children. There is no indication that she knew or could have known anything more than she recounted. What she failed to do was to accept the mistaken allegation of rape and to aid the Bureau in its exploration of this suspicion. According to petitioner, the parents "refused to believe that their child had been raped. They stated that they would not go into any conversation about rape with their children. They explained that in their country, a child did not learn about sex until the child was about 15 years of age; nor did the mother want me to discuss this with the child."

No doubt Mrs. Vulon's perturbation (described by petitioner) about the erroneous rape theory was due in part to the great damage that this charge would have inflicted on Maurice, the only suspect, who was an exemplary student in a Catholic school, aspiring to the priesthood. Though Mrs. Vulon apparently was herself concerned and frustrated that she was unable to ascertain the exact source of Michelle's bleeding, it was to the benefit rather than the detriment of her children that she refused to succumb to the mistaken suspicion of rape or to give it further currency.

Petitioner's attorney argued that neglect should be inferred from the parental failure to explain the basis for Michelle's bleeding. . . .

Prosecution of this petition was largely attributable, it is clear, to the parents' refusal of the Bureau's request that they consent to their children's examination by the Court psychiatrist. Such examination apparently was viewed in part by the Bureau as a possible method of determining whether Maurice committed the non-existent rape. So intent was the Bureau on its proposal that its attorney approached the Court ex parte before the hearing to ask it to order such examinations.

. . . The Vulons believe that their children's welfare will not be served by probing into the frightening episode of Michelle's bleeding by social workers or psychiatrists, and indeed indicate that the repetitive references to the incident to which the children have already been subjected were detrimental.

* * *

This Court believes from observation of these parents and children that they have an affectionate, mutually-respecting and beneficial relationship. A good faith appraisal by responsible and concerned parents, such as the Vulons, of the best way to handle a problem of child development on which reasonable men can differ in their value judgments, is not neglect. . . . While it was necessary and proper to conduct some investigation of whether Michelle's unusual condition indicated abuse or lack of care, the State cannot, without more justification than here appears, override the liberty of the parents, protected by the Constitution, to bring up their children as they think best. . . .

Petition dismissed.[15]

Under our ground for intervention there would not be, as there was even for Judge Dembitz, probable cause to invoke the process, to investigate the Vulon family. There would have been no report by the attending physician to a state agency.[16] Indeed, the confidentiality of the relationship between parent, patient, and doctor is to be safeguarded. This ground should be seen as an inducement to parents whose children have been injured to provide them with medical care—thus eliminating a deterrent to do so because of the fear of being reported for neglect or abuse. Laws requiring physicians, nurses, social workers, and educators to report suspected cases have contributed little to protecting children.*

Finally, the ground we next propose takes into account the optional additional element in the American Bar Association's definition of sexual abuse: "and is seriously harmed physically or emotionally thereby." The next ground covers serious physical harm, whether

---

* Mandatory reporting has swelled the number of complaints for neglect and abuse that must be investigated by the state.[17] In most states a third or more of these complaints are for alleged neglect that does not involve imminent risk of serious bodily injury. Investigations in such cases frequently constitute an unwarranted intrusion into family privacy, weakening the integrity of the families involved. Two thirds of the mandated reports are for alleged physical or sexual abuse or for children at imminent risk of serious bodily injury. Coercive inquiries follow even when the state does not have adequate homemakers, social workers, psychiatric, emergency, foster, medical care, or other backup services.[18] The overbroad and vague base for mandatory reporting and inquiry has led to overreporting, to unnecessary demands on services that are inadequate even for those children at greatest risk of serious bodily injury. Thus, those already at serious risk are put at greater risk, and damaging coercive intrusion is encouraged into families of children whose needs, if real, can best be served—and perhaps can only be served—by a range of voluntary services that would be available, accessible, and attractive to families who are or tend to be disorganized.[19]

or not sexually related, and rejects "harmed emotionally" as too vague and imprecise to justify coercive intrusion.

SERIOUS BODILY INJURY INFLICTED BY PARENTS UPON THEIR CHILD, AN ATTEMPT TO INFLICT SUCH INJURY, OR THE REPEATED FAILURE OF PARENTS TO PREVENT THEIR CHILD FROM SUFFERING SUCH INJURY SHOULD BE A GROUND FOR INTERVENTION

This ground for intervention is designed to establish a minimum standard of care below which no parents may go without losing their exclusive right to raise their children. It is meant to give the state the authority to identify and to provide protection to children who are brutally kicked, beaten, or attacked by their parents.[20] It is meant to safeguard children whose parents may have attempted to injure them, for example, by starvation, poisoning, or strangling. Finally, it is designed to safeguard children from parents who prove to be incapable of preventing their child from repeatedly suffering serious bodily injury or from being exposed to such harm.

This ground rests upon a recognition that among the many functions which a young child cannot fulfill for himself is care for his own body, notably its protection from serious harm. The risks which a child courts usually stem from his developmental inability not only to judge what is dangerous, but also to take over responsibility for safeguarding his body. A young child's enjoyment of adventuresome, impulsive behavior far outstrips his capacity to appraise the consequences. Even after listening to and apparently understanding repeated parental warnings, children are still apt to run into heavy traffic, spill boiling water on themselves, or eat poisonous substances. The child's lack of regard for the safety of his body becomes the concern of his parents, who normally value and protect it as they would their own. It takes years before this state of affairs changes, before the child identifies with his parents' attitudes and begins to "look after himself."

When parents do not act according to this expectation, when they inflict or attempt to inflict serious bodily injury, or when they repeatedly fail to protect their child from such bodily harm, the state must be authorized to intervene. It should provide substitute parents or, in the event of repeated unintended injuries, the supportive assistance essential to the child's future safety. Supportive help would permit families to remain together and would be preferred as the least intrusive, least emotionally damaging disposition. Such dispositions, however, are inappropriate for the battered child whose injuries are inflicted by his parents. Parental maltreatment leaves psychological scars which endure long beyond any physical healing and preclude a child from regaining the feeling of being safe, wanted, and cared for in his parents' presence—the very emotions on which his further developmental advances need to be based.[21]

This ground's "serious bodily injury" standard excludes intervention for the many minor assaults on the child's body which go under the name of corporal punishment. We acknowledge that some parents, un-

aware of their child's vulnerability, regard the infliction of physical pain as an indispensable deterrent in
the disciplining of their child. As psychoanalysts and
educators we condemn these as harmful, humiliating,
and, in general, injurious to the child's development.
The abolition of corporal punishment by parents is,
however, not a matter for legislation but for the gradual
enlightenment and humanizing of public attitudes as
a whole.[22]

By restricting intervention to a "serious bodily
injury" standard, this ground is also meant to give fair
warning to parents. Serious damage to any part of the
child's body surface, his bone structure, or his organ
systems reveals itself even to an untrained observer by
the child's pain, by visible signs, or by change in body
function. Medical opinion is sufficiently in agreement
and diagnostic skills are sufficiently advanced to determine the causes of most injuries, both traumatic and
toxic. Furthermore, this ground is meant to protect
families from the unwarranted intrusions authorized
by neglect statutes that use such undefined terms as
"denial of proper care," "psychological abuse," or
"serious emotional damage." [23] These terms are too
vague to restrain state authorities who have come to
exercise coercive power based on a wide range of child-
rearing notions about which there is neither professional nor societal consensus.*

---

* The test of mental health is to be found not in any particular style of life, but in the absence of serious internal conflicts—
in the harmony of inner agencies. Evaluations of a child, or for that
matter of an adult, which simply equate social compliance with
mental health and noncompliance with mental illness are wrong.

IMPLICATIONS

EMOTIONAL NEGLECT

Though the "serious bodily injury" ground, like our other grounds for intervention, is concerned with emotional repercussions on the child, it is defined solely in terms of physical harm. It authorizes the termination of relationships with parents who seriously injure their child—not only because of the physical harm but also because they have destroyed his trust in them. Like our other justifications for intervention, this ground is designed to minimize the psychological abuse of children by the *state,* when it coercively intrudes for such vaguely conceived reasons as "unfit home," "parental conduct detrimental to mental health," "emotional neglect," or "emotional harm." These are too imprecise, in terms of definition, cause, treatment, and consequences, to ensure fair warning and thus adequate control over judges, lawyers, police, social workers, and other participants in the child placement process.

The requisites for intrusion are not met even by the elaborate language of the American Bar Association's efforts to resolve the problem of defining "emotional neglect." Its ground justifies intervention for serious emotional damage as evidenced by a child's "severe anxiety, depression, or withdrawal, or untoward aggressive behavior toward self or others." [24] But observed behavior is not enough for assessing a child's mental state. What appears to be similar behavior, whether as a symptom of illness or a sign of health, may for different persons be a response to a wide range of different and even opposite psychic factors. And the same deep-seated emotional disturbance may lead to the most diverse manifestations in a child's behavior.

The causes of the surface symptom of "severe anxiety" may range from the rational (for example, fear of extreme violence witnessed in the parental home) to the severely neurotic (for example, the child's fear of being overwhelmed by his own sexual or aggressive impulses). Likewise, what the Bar Association calls "depression or withdrawal" may be the result of environmental circumstances: it may stem from the absence of appropriate persons for emotional attachment; from the lack of stimulation that leaves the child uninterested in the world outside and predominantly interested in his own body as a source of excitation and tension discharge; or it may be the initial sign of a child's intrinsic abnormality such as an autistic or psychotic process. Similarly, a child may betray "untoward aggressive behavior toward self and others" for a wide variety of reasons: because he was born with a particularly strong aggressive drive; because in his infancy he was deprived of the affection which should have aroused his loving feelings and toned down his aggression; because he was treated harshly by his parents and identified with their aggressive attitudes; because he was exposed to deprivations which were intolerable and aroused aggressive responses in him; or because his moral standards, once acquired, forbade aggression to be directed against the outside world and left it to be turned against his own person.

We recognize that emotional disorders are serious threats to any child's healthy progress toward adulthood. But there can be no comparable certainty that the attitudes or the action or inaction of the parents cause these damaging symptoms in the same way that we can be certain of the origins of physical injury. A child can become emotionally disturbed in response to parental attitudes, to fateful events, to a combination of these, or entirely because of internal or inborn factors.

The variety of opinions concerning causes is reflected in a similar lack of consensus concerning treatment, treatability, and prognosis. The Bar Association's ground is therefore not improved by its restricting coercive intervention to those situations in which parents refuse treatment for their child's "serious emotional damage." [25] Indeed, psychological therapy for a young child is not likely to be useful and sustained without the parents' willing, not forced, cooperation.

In the face of these uncertainties and imprecise definitions of "emotional neglect" and "serious emotional damage," neither concept should be used as a ground for modifying or terminating parent-child relationships. Even if "emotional neglect" could be precisely defined, recognition of how little we know about the "right" treatment, and how little consensus there is about treatments, should caution against using the power of the state to intrude.* Thus, in cases such as those involving the infant *Shay, Richard,* and the *Alsager* children, there would be no justification for state intervention—even if it were limited to making an inquiry.

---

* This position should not obscure the need for state-supported voluntary services for assisting parents to identify and deal with their child's emotional needs.

Miss *Shay,* a 22-year-old unmarried "hippy," as she neared the end of an uneventful pregnancy, decided to keep her baby, having initially expressed the wish to have it adopted. The hospital social worker reported to the state's protective services that there was reason to feel worried about the child's safety and well-being because of Miss Shay's change of mind about adoption and because she was eccentric in her attire as well as her attitude toward food and cleanliness.

The baby and mother had a normal labor and birth experience and left the hospital for their one-room apartment a few days later. The protective services worker called on Miss Shay after neighbors reported that she was "acting in a peculiar manner." The peculiarities observed by the neighbors and confirmed by the worker's investigation included: "(1) Miss Shay fed the baby by leaning over the crib side and breast-feeding with the baby in the supine position; (2) Miss Shay cut a hole in the mattress with a pail below and did not use diapers on the baby when the baby was in her crib." In addition, the neighbors said that they were upset because Miss Shay had been throwing all the knives from her apartment into the trash; they feared she would harm the baby with a knife.

Miss Shay's "peculiar behavior" was of considerable concern to the protective services. In order to have time to discuss with the mother how babies should be cared for, the social worker "convinced" her that it would be desirable to hospitalize the child for observation in the ward for abused and neglected children—even though, in the opinion of the baby's doctor and the public health nurse, the infant girl was "well nourished and behaving normally." One evening, fearful of losing her child, the mother took the baby and walked out of the hospital. Unable to find public transportation, she began hitchhiking home with the baby in her arms. The police picked them up on the road.

The child care agency then placed the baby in a distant hospital and refused to tell Miss Shay where her daughter was until it could be determined whether the baby was a "neglected child." The state's statute provided that "a child may be found 'neglected' who ... is being denied proper care and attention, physically, educationally, emotionally or is being permitted to live under conditions, circumstances or associations injurious to his well-being. . . ."

Two weeks later the social worker petitioned the court to place the baby under the guardianship of the Welfare Commissioner. The court granted the petition, and the 2-month-old infant was placed in a foster home.[26]

Under the grounds that we propose no such intrusiveness would have been permitted. Even the initial inquiries would not have been justified.

Richard, the son of Miss Margaret Wambles, a 25-year-old white woman, was born in September 1971 and lived with her continuously until June 1975 when he was seized by a Montgomery, Alabama, policeman and placed in the custody of the Welfare Department, pending an adjudication of "neglected child." Following a complaint by the putative father, this emergency placement was ordered by Judge Thetford of the Family

Court under the authority of a statute which defined "neglected child" as any child under 16 years of age who "has no proper parental care . . . or whose home . . . is an unfit and improper place for such child . . . or who for any other cause is in need of the care and protection of the state" and which provided for emergency placement without a hearing "if it appears from the petition that . . . the child is in such condition that its welfare requires that custody be immediately assumed. . . ."

After obtaining a pickup order, three police officers went to Miss Wambles's home at 8:30 in the evening and announced that they had come to take Richard into custody.[27] According to the deposition of one of the police officers:

> A.   She picked Richard up and ran back to the back of the house.
>
> Q.   What did you do?
>
> A.   I chased after her.

* * *

> Q.   And where was Richard?
>
> A.   He was in Margaret's arms.

* * *

> Q.   What kind of emotional state was Margaret in?
>
> A.   She was screaming — not screaming, but she was fussing and raising a disturbance. She was — she appeared to be upset.

Q. And what about the child?

A. He was — he was upset.

Q. Okay. By "upset," can you explain what you mean by that? Was he crying?

A. He was more of a — it was more of a look of what's going on, you know. He was looking at his mother and he was looking at me and couldn't — it was more of a confusion type of thing.

Q. Did he make any noise?

A. He did when Margaret started saying, "No, you are not going to take him." He said, "No, Mama, don't let him take me."

* * *

Q. What happened then?

A. I grabbed her by the arm and pulled her back into the living room where it was lighted. It was dark in the hall.

* * *

Q. Were you holding her tightly?

A. I was holding [her arm] so that she would not be able to pull loose and run or anything like this. I advised her that non-compliance with this pick-up order could result in her going to jail because this was a court order.

* * *

Q. What happened then?

A. [S]he handed the child over to me and I gave her the court order to read. . . .

Q. What kind of state was she in at this point?

A. Nervous; she was shaking.

* * *

Q. [W]hat state was Richard in after he was handed to you?

A. He was rather confused — he didn't quite — could not figure out what was going on.* [28]

"The only facts about Margaret Wambles known to Judge Thetford before he issued the pick-up order were that she was unemployed and that she and her child are white and were living with a black man in a black neighborhood. Judge Thetford had no information as to how long Margaret Wambles had lived in Montgomery, where she had worked, or how long she had been unemployed. He had no evidence that Richard . . . was being physically abused and no information as to the condition of the Wambles' home. Judge Thetford knew nothing about the man with whom Margaret Wambles was living, other than his race and the fact that he was not married to her. Judge Thetford testified that the race of the man with whom Plaintiff Wambles was living was relevant to his decision to order Richard . . . removed from his mother's custody, particularly because they were living in a black neighborhood. Judge Thet-

---

* Not only from a child's point of view, but from an adult's as well, there is no rational explanation for what was going on.

ford concluded that this habitation in a black neighborhood could be dangerous for a child because it was his belief that 'it was not a healthy thing for a white child to be the only [white] child in a black neighborhood.' "[29]

Under the grounds for intervention that we propose, no petition for modification or termination of parental rights could have been entertained. The finding of "neglected child" and termination of Richard's right to his mother would have been precluded. Indeed, just as in the *Shay* case and the *Alsager* case which follows, no emergency placement could have been ordered since there was no cause for believing that the child's physical well-being was seriously threatened.

In the spring of 1969 the probation department in Des Moines, Iowa, received a number of complaints from neighbors about the children of Charles and Darlene *Alsager*. At that time they had been married 11 years and were the parents of six children: George, 10; Wanda, 8; John, 7; Charles Jr., 6; Michael, 4; and Albert, who was less than 1 year old.[30] Various neighbors wrote to the probation authorities: "The oldest boy . . . does nasty things with his little sister, Wanda. . . . The children cuss me and throw rocks at me and at the house and car and at my daughter. . . . [Mrs. Alsager's mother] cusses and swears and carries on something terrible over the phone if you call them about the children. . . . We appeal to you to help us to place the children and this family where they belong. We have taken care of them long enough." [31]

On the basis of such complaints and under the authority of Iowa's child neglect statute, Jane Johnston, a probation officer, was instructed by her superiors to invoke the process—to investigate the Alsager family. The statute provided for the termination of parent-child relationships if "the parents have . . . repeatedly refused to give the child necessary parental care and protection" or "if the parents are unfit by reason of . . . conduct found by the court likely to be detrimental to the physical or mental health or morals of the child." On June 20, 1969, officer Johnston "visited" the Alsager home. She "spent approximately twenty minutes inside the Alsager residence, which at the time was occupied only by Mrs. Alsager and the baby, Albert. Based on her observations inside the house, and without seeing the other five children, Miss Johnston determined that all six children should immediately be removed to the Polk County Juvenile Home. This removal was to be temporary, pending a hearing to determine whether the children were 'neglected.' . . ." [32]

As a result of the adjudication hearing which took place within a week after the children were taken from their parents, District Judge Tidrick found the children to be neglected. The evidence revealed "that the Alsagers sometimes permitted their children to leave the house in cold weather without winter clothing on, 'allowed them' to play in traffic, to annoy neighbors, to eat mush for supper, to live in a house containing dirty dishes and laundry, and to sometimes arrive late at school. At the time of the termination, Mr. Alsager was a working man who had never been on public welfare rolls. He and his wife lived together, and shared an interest in keeping their family unit intact." [33]

In May 1970, after the Alsager children had been

out of their home for almost a year, Judge Tidrick terminated the parental rights of Charles and Darlene Alsager "in and to" five of their six children. By 1974, these five children had experienced between them more than "15 separate foster home placements, and eight juvenile home placements." [34]

Under the grounds we propose, the state action which destroyed the Alsager family would have been precluded. There was not even enough evidence to justify an inquiry, let alone an emergency placement and termination of parental rights.

If "emotional neglect" or "serious emotional damage" is to be the basis of any ground for action in a child placement code, it should be used to hold the state accountable for its violations of family integrity. The state should not be immune when it exceeds the authority delegated to it by the grounds for intervention. Had our grounds been adopted at the time of their actions, the authorities in the *Shay* case, the *Wambles* case, and the *Alsager* case would have been liable for the emotional neglect or psychological abuse of the infant Shay; of Richard; and of George, Wanda, John, Charles Jr., Michael, and Albert Alsager.

As we now turn to a series of cases that illustrate circumstances which would justify state intervention under the serious-bodily-injury ground, the strange paradox which characterizes child placement law becomes evident. While the state in the preceding cases was too intrusive, it was not intrusive enough in at least two of the three cases that are discussed in the next section. Indeed, because of its failure to terminate parent-child relationships in the *Vigora* and *Gray* cases, the state also ought to be held liable.[35]

CHILD ABUSE AND NEGLECT

The provision in this ground for intervention concerned with the *infliction* of serious bodily injury would have applied to the case of Norman *Vigora*. In June 1971, Norman was admitted to the hospital with "contusions on his right eye, skull, lumbar spine and both shoulders." His parents had beaten him because "he was fussy and cried too much." * Upon his release from the hospital, the court ordered him placed in emergency foster care with the Wilsons, his aunt and uncle. The judge urged the Vigoras to seek counseling and encouraged them to visit Norman regularly.

Norman remained in uninterrupted care with the Wilsons for 4½ years. During this period the Vigoras visited him on an average of once every 2 weeks and tried to prepare him and themselves for his return. In 1975, shortly after the birth of another child, they brought suit to revoke the foster placement order. The

---

* A young child's behavior is experienced differently by various adults or by the same adult at different times according to differing moods. For example: (1) Parents may experience their child's fussy behavior as normative; they will rock, soothe, and stay with the child patiently. (2) Parents may experience such behavior as illness in the child and call the pediatrician or discuss it with the visiting nurse. (3) Parents may experience the fussy behavior as violently and provocatively demanding, and react to it by the need to "survive"—not allowing the "tyrannical" baby to destroy them. The helplessness of the infant is a magnet for nurture, for attention, and for action; it is also a painful reminder to the adult of his own earlier helplessness and, perversely, can be a magnet for attack.

court requested an evaluation of the Vigoras, Norman, and the Wilsons, who were eager to have the child become a permanent member of their family. The evaluations revealed that Norman, then aged 5½, was preoccupied with being taken away from the Wilsons. When the Vigoras would tell him of their hope that he would be moving to live with them and his "new baby sister," he became confused and fearful. He resumed bed-wetting, which had stopped when he was 2½.

Nothing in the evaluation suggested that the Vigoras were unfit to take care of their second child. But the Vigoras could never be adequate parents for Norman—not only because they might physically abuse him again, but because there was no way for him to feel safe in their care. The Vigoras argued that all they wanted was "another chance to be Norman's parents and that if they screwed up again then the courts could take him away permanently." [36]

Under this ground for intervention, the Vigoras would have been denied a second chance following the adjudication in 1971 that they had inflicted serious bodily injury on Norman.*

The provision in this ground for intervention that is concerned with *attempts* to inflict serious bodily injury would have terminated the legal relationship between Ruth *Gray* and her two children, Dawn and Todd, ages 4 and 6. Mrs. Gray was given custody of the

* Even if there had been no history of child beating, under the longtime caretaker ground in Chapter 4 Norman would have been eligible for a permanent place in the Wilson family as far back as 1973.

children when the Grays were divorced in 1965. Mr. Gray remarried. Several months later, Mrs. Gray attempted to kill the children and herself. After carefully preparing the gas range in the kitchen with a plastic enclosure to collect the fumes, Mrs. Gray drugged herself and her children and placed them under the plastic. A last-minute call to a neighbor resulted in their rescue. When the children were released from the hospital, their father and his second wife assumed responsibility for their care. Mrs. Gray was indicted for assault with intent to murder and was found not guilty by reason of insanity. She was committed to a psychiatric hospital in 1966. The court declared that the children should be available for liberal visitation by the mother whenever her psychiatrist felt she was well enough to visit. Later, after the mother was discharged in 1968, the court extended the visitation order to include overnight visits.

Adoption, sought by the stepmother, would have followed an adjudication of attempted serious bodily injury under our ground for intervention. But it was denied by the court because Ruth Gray refused consent. Once again, she was granted visitation rights. Both children had extreme reactions of fear for their lives when they were told their mother would be visiting. The night before each visit, which the father insisted should take place under his supervision, the children were upset, physically and psychologically. Todd took a clublike piece of wood to bed with him to protect himself and resumed bed-wetting. Dawn had nightmares, stomachaches, and diarrhea. Both children were stiff, pale, and unable to relax in their mother's company. They repeatedly asked their father for protection, fear-ing that if they accepted food or drink or were alone with her, she would try to kill them. Over and over they asked their parents to keep her from killing them.[37]

These children were preoccupied with saving their lives. Their fears and anxiety were anchored in reality. Despite this, the court remained convinced that the mother's blood ties to the children justified enforcing her "right" to them.

Even in a legal system that generally requires visits in custody awards, our ground would prohibit the state from forcing these two children to see their mother. Todd and Dawn would be entitled to be adopted by their stepmother and thus to feel secure in their family.*

Under the provision of the ground that is concerned with the *repeated failure* of parents *to prevent* their child from suffering serious bodily injury, the relationship between Donald *Carlson* and his mother would be modified. In November 1970, during a routine school physical examination, Donald, age 10, was diagnosed as having juvenile diabetes mellitus. He was immediately hospitalized because he was dehydrated and his blood sugar level was very high. During the 16-day period of Donald's hospitalization, Mrs. Carlson received instructions from hospital nurses and dieticians on how to manage his diabetes. Yet in December Donald was hospitalized again for hypoglycemic reaction due to her inability to provide proper diet and insulin control. The hospital staff tried to help her understand

* Father and stepmother would have qualified as longtime caretakers by this time. See Chapter 4.

what was required. But Donald had to be hospitalized again in March 1971 because of his mother's repeated failure, despite her cooperative spirit and good intentions, to manage his need to observe a special diet, take insulin shots, and follow a schedule of exercise and rest. This repeated failure of parental care constituted a threat to Donald's physical well-being and life. The least intrusive disposition—one that would have minimized the stress on Donald's psychological tie to his mother—would have been to provide a family helper. If Mrs. Carlson could have cooperated, the helper could have managed Donald's medical care and special diet.* Unfortunately, that disposition was not an available alternative. Thus, in order to protect Donald's life, he was placed in foster care where his diabetes is under control. He has required no further hospitalization.[38]

Unlike the ground of repeated failures to prevent serious bodily injury, the ground for intervention we discuss in the next chapter is concerned with state supervention of parental judgments about the provision of specific medical interventions.

---

* In accord with the principle of the least intrusive intervention, the role of the family helper would be generally limited to meeting the specific need that was established in the adjudication of the ground for intervention.

Chapter 6

Refusal by Parents to Authorize Lifesaving Medical Care

REFUSAL BY PARENTS TO AUTHORIZE MEDICAL CARE WHEN (1) MEDICAL EXPERTS AGREE THAT TREATMENT IS NONEXPERIMENTAL AND APPROPRIATE FOR THE CHILD, AND (2) DENIAL OF THAT TREATMENT WOULD RESULT IN DEATH, AND (3) THE ANTICIPATED RESULT OF TREATMENT IS WHAT SOCIETY WOULD WANT FOR EVERY CHILD—A CHANCE FOR NORMAL HEALTHY GROWTH OR A LIFE WORTH LIVING—SHOULD BE A GROUND FOR INTERVENTION

Under this ground, state supervention of parental judgment would be justified to provide any proven, non-experimental medical procedure when its denial would mean death for a child who would otherwise have an opportunity for either a life worth living or a life of relatively normal healthy growth. While a life of relatively normal healthy growth is assumed to be a life worth living, it is not assumed that all lives worth living from a societal-consensus point of view could be characterized as relatively normal or healthy. For example, society might view the life of a quadraplegic child, in need of a blood transfusion for reasons unrelated to that condition, as a "life worth living," though not one of normal healthy growth. Thus the state would overcome the presumption of parental autonomy if it could establish: (a) that the medical profession is in agreement about what nonexperimental medical treatment is appropriate for the child; (b) that the denial of the treatment would mean death for the child; and (c) that the expected outcome of that treatment is what society agrees to be right for any child—a chance for normal healthy growth or a life worth living.*

Under this ground, when death is not a likely consequence of exercising a medical choice, there would be no justification for governmental intrusion. Where the question involves not a life-or-death choice but a preference for one style of life over another, the law must restrain courts and doctors from coercively imposing their personal preferences in the form of medical care upon nonconsenting parents and their children.

This ground acknowledges that parents normally protect their child's body as if it were their own and that parents generally have the capacity to make

* Nothing in this ground would preclude parents from seeking or consenting to treatment on behalf of a child who society does not think could ever have a life worth living.

health care choices for their children. Further, it recognizes that the law cannot find in medicine (or, for that matter, in any science) the ethical, political, or social values for evaluating health care choices.*

In its commitment to family integrity this ground does not take a simplistic view of parents, of the parent-child relationship, or of the family. Rather, it acknowledges not only man's complexity, but also the law's limited capacity for making more than gross distinctions about human needs, natures, and patterns of development. This ground recognizes and respects the diverse range of man's religious, cultural, scientific, and ethical beliefs and the overlapping and ever-changing modes of their expression within and between generations at all stages of the life cycle. Thus, a prime function of law is to prevent one person's truth (here about health and the good life) from becoming another person's tyranny.

This ground does not justify coercive intrusion by the state in those life-or-death situations in which (a) there is no proven medical procedure; *or* (b) there is conflicting medical advice about which, if any, treatment procedure to follow; † *or* (c) there is less than a high probability that the nonexperimental treatment will enable the child to have either a life worth living

* Courts must avoid confusing a doctor's personal preference with the scientific bases upon which the recommendation rests.[1]

† If there is a conflict about which proven treatment to follow, but failure to consent to one of the proven treatments would result in the child's death *and* denial of a life worth living or relatively normal healthy growth (see c), the state would be authorized to order that one of the proven treatments be undertaken.

or a life of relatively normal healthy growth, even if the medical experts agree about treatment.[2]

The requisite elements of this ground are intended to place strict limits upon the authority of the state to intervene. In their evidentiary demands and limited scope these elements saddle the state with the burden of overcoming the presumption of parental autonomy. Parents remain free to provide medical treatment which the state could not impose.

Outside a narrow central core of agreement, "a life worth living" and "a life of relatively normal healthy growth" are highly personal terms about which there is no societal consensus. There can thus be no societal consensus about the "rightness" of always deciding for "life," or always preferring the predicted result of the recommended treatment over the predicted result of refusing such treatment. Those cases in which reasonable and responsible persons can and do disagree about whether the "life" after treatment will be "worth living" or "normal," and thus about what is "right," are precisely those in which parents must remain free of coercive state intervention in deciding whether to reject or consent to the medical program offered to their child.

No one has a greater right or responsibility, nor can anyone be presumed to be in a better position, than a child's parents to decide what course to pursue if the medical experts disagree about treatment.[3] The same is true if there is no general agreement in society that the outcome of a proven treatment is clearly preferable to the outcome of no treatment. Put somewhat more starkly, how can parents in such situations be judged to give the wrong answer when there is no way of knowing the right answer? In these circumstances, if the law's guarantee of freedom of belief is to be meaningful, parents must have the right to act on their belief within the privacy of their family. The burden must always be on the state to establish what is wrong and not on parents to establish that what may be right for them is necessarily right for others.

Unlike the ground of repeated failure to prevent serious bodily injury, this ground is concerned with unacceptable parental judgments about specific medical interventions. While serious bodily injury justifies changes in custody, this ground authorizes only a disposition limited to the medical intervention that is ordered. It otherwise leaves the child in the general overall care and custody of his parents and restores him to it as quickly as possible.

IMPLICATIONS

WHEN DEATH IS AN ISSUE

The criteria for intervention under this ground were met for Judge Murphy of the Superior Court of the District of Columbia in *In re Pogue*.[4] He authorized blood transfusions for an otherwise healthy newborn infant who would have died had his parents' decision to reject the treatment been honored. At the same time, recognizing the distinction between an adult and a child with regard to medical care choices, Judge Murphy declined to order blood transfusions for the infant's mother, who in the face of death refused to consent to such intervention. Over the objection of the "adult" parents' wishes and of course without regard to the infant's "wishes," Judge Murphy decided as a substitute parent to protect the child's right to reach the age of majority—when he will become entitled to make such life-or-death decisions for himself. The judge implicitly found the infant's parents temporarily incompetent to care for their child. Simultaneously, he acknowledged that the mother's adult status entitled her to decide to refuse blood for herself.

The scientific "fact" that the death of both was inevitable without transfusion—the nonexperimental medical procedure—was not in dispute. Nor was there any societal doubt about the desirability, the "rightness" of the predicted outcome of the transfusion: an opportunity for normal, healthy growth, a life worth living. The issue was whether the judge and doctors who shared an unqualified value preference for life could use the power of the state to impose their "adult" judgment on others whose own "adult" judgment gave greater weight to another preference. On behalf of the adult the answer was "No"; on behalf of the child the answer was "Yes." Thus, coercive intervention by the state was justified. Otherwise the parents' decision would have deprived a child of proven medical treatment and consequently of an opportunity to reach adulthood when a person is free of parental control and presumed competent to decide for himself.

But this ground would let parents decide, for another example, whether their congenitally malformed newborn with an ascertainable neurological deficiency and highly predictable mental retardation should be provided with treatment which might avoid death, yet which offered no chance of cure. Dr. Raymond Duff has argued persuasively:

> Families know their values, priorities and resources better than anyone else. Presumably they, with the doctor, can make the better choices as a private affair. Certainly, they, more than anyone else, must live with the consequences. . . . If they cannot cope adequately with the child and their other responsibilities and survive as a family, they may feel that the death option is a forced choice. . . . But that is not necessarily bad, and who knows of a better way? [5]

If parental autonomy is not accorded recognition and if society insists through law that such children, indeed any children, receive medical treatment rejected by their parents, the state must take upon itself the burden of providing the special financial, physical, and psychological resources essential to making real the value it prefers for the child it "saves." The state would have to demonstrate its capacity for making such "unwanted" children "wanted" ones. Minimally, it should fully finance their special-care requirements. In the event parents do not wish to remain responsible for their child, the state would have to find—what is rarely available—adopting parents or other caretakers who can meet not only the child's physical needs but also his psychological requirements for affectionate relationships and emotional and intellectual stimulation.*

---

* Except for meeting the child's physical needs, however, the task is beyond the limits of law, no matter how large the allo-

No matter how limited their potential for healthy growth and development, such children demand and deserve affection and the opportunity to develop psychological ties that institutional arrangements do not provide.[6] As long as the state offers institutions that provide little more than storage space and "hay, oats, and water"[7] for these children, the law must err on the side of the strong presumption in favor of parental autonomy. The state must therefore *either assume* full responsibility for the treatment, care, and nurture of such children, *or honor* the parents' decision to consent to or refuse treatment.

The case of Karen, a teen-ager suffering from irreversible kidney malfunction, provides another life-or-death example in which the standard of an opportunity for a life worth living or a life of relatively normal healthy growth toward adulthood would preclude state supervention of parental judgments. Karen's case poses the question of whether state intervention should be authorized to review the choice of an adolescent who, with her parent's permission and concurrence, decides to choose death over "life." Following an unsuccessful kidney transplant, Karen and her parents refused to consent to the continuation of "intolerable" life-support devices. The decision to proceed as if family privacy and parental autonomy were protected was described in an article by her doctors:

---

cation of financial resources. The law is too crude an instrument to nurture, as only parents can, the delicate physical, psychological, and social tissues of a child's life.

[F]ollowing the transplant's failure, thrice-weekly hemodialysis was performed. Karen tolerated dialysis poorly, routinely having chills, nausea, vomiting, severe headaches and weakness. . . .

[A]fter it was clear that the kidney would never function, Karen and her parents expressed the wish to stop medical treatment and let "nature take its course." . . . [S]taff members conveyed to the family that such wishes were unheard of and unacceptable, and that a decision to stop treatment could never be an alternative. The family did decide to continue dialysis, medication, and diet therapy. Karen's renal incapacity returned to pretransplant levels and she returned to her socially isolated life, diet restriction, chronic discomfort, and fatigue.

On May 10, Karen was hospitalized following ten days of high fever. Three days later the transplant was removed. Its pathology resembled that of the original kidneys, and the possibility of a similar reaction forming in subsequent transplants was established.

On May 21, the arteriovenous shunt placed in Karen's arm for hemodialysis was found to be infected, and part of the vein wall was excised and the shunt revised. During this portion of the hospitalization, Karen and the parents grudgingly went along with the medical recommendations, but they continued to ponder the possibility of stopping treatment. . . . On May 24, the shunt clotted closed. Karen, with her parents' agreement, refused shunt revision and any further dialysis. . . .

Karen died on June 2, with both parents at her bedside. . . .[8]

For Karen and her parents, no medical treatment offered the possibility for her to resume a life worth living. The insistence of the nursing and medical staff to continue the life-support system was not a scientific, but a value choice. The rightness of forcing the consequences of their choice upon Karen rather than honoring her and her parents' decision could not be established. There was therefore no basis for exercising the power of the state to supervene the judgment of Karen's parents. Had Karen been an adult on the law's chronological scale, there is no question, or there ought not to be, that out of respect for her dignity as a human being the doctors would have had to abide by her request to end treatment.

Had the situation been different, had Karen's parents insisted, over her objection, on continuing the life-support system, would the state have been justified in supervening their judgment? The answer is "No." Had Karen insisted over her parent's objection on continuing the life-support system, would the state have been justified in supervening their judgment? The answer is "Yes"—if the state provides, as it must, whatever resources are required to assure full care for the child.* But if the state will not provide such support, the answer is an uneasy "No." It is, after all, the func-

* Because a few parents might not follow a child's express wish to undergo treatment which might seem intolerable to them,

tion and responsibility of parents to evaluate and make judgments about the wishes and requests of their children. The meaning of parental autonomy is that parents make such decisions. Further, neither court nor agency is likely to be as competent as were Karen's parents to determine her capacity for choice and whether to abide by it. The law should avoid giving the discretion for such subjective judgments to its agents.

WHEN DEATH IS NOT AN ISSUE

Where death is not in issue, this ground is intended to preclude a decision such as that in *In re Sampson*.[10] That case illustrates how vague neglect statutes may be invoked in the name of health care to violate a family's privacy, to undermine parental autonomy, and to foster a community's or judge's prejudice against the physically deformed. Under the Family Court Act of New York, Judge Elwyn declared 15-year-old Kevin Sampson "a neglected child." He made this finding in order to establish his authority to veto a decision by Kevin's mother not to force her son to undergo a series of operations which had been recommended by the Commissioner of Health and by duly qualified surgeons to correct a facial condition called

though not to their child, the law might reinforce society's general commitment to life by recognizing in life-death situations any child's express wish for treatment against the parents' wishes. Alternatively, legislatures might develop a formula for emancipation which defines the circumstances and sets an age below majority when children may become their own risk-takers for all or some specific health care decisions.[9] Without a statutory formula, the ultimate responsibility must remain with parents who may or may not decide to support their child's choice.

neurofibromatosis. Judge Elwyn observed that Kevin had "a massive deformity of the right side of his face and neck. The outward manifestation of the disease is a large fold or flap of an overgrowth of facial tissue which causes the whole cheek, the corner of his mouth and right ear to drop down giving him an appearance which can only be described as grotesque and repulsive." Judge Elwyn went on to psychologize and predict:

> [T]he massive deformity of the entire right side of his face and neck is patently so gross and so disfiguring that it must inevitably exert a most negative effect upon his personality development, his opportunity for education and later employment and upon every phase of his relationship with his peers and others.[11]

Judge Elwyn made his assertion even though he acknowledged that "the staff psychiatrist of the County Mental Health Center reported that 'there is no evidence of any thinking disorder' and that 'in spite of marked facial disfigurement he failed to show any outstanding personality aberration.' " "Nevertheless," the judge added, "this finding hardly justifies a conclusion that he has been or will continue to be wholly unaffected by his misfortune."[12] He also noted that Kevin had been exempted from school not because he was intellectually incapable, but, it may be assumed, because he appeared to his classmates and teachers, as he did to Judge Elwyn himself, "grotesque and repulsive." But the judge's speculations on behalf of the state as *parens patriae* did not lead him to consider that under the protective cloak of family privacy, a loving, accepting, autonomous parent had been able to nurture in Kevin a "healthy personality." Kevin, after all, had so developed in spite of state-reinforced prejudice and discrimination in school, health agency, and court against the cosmetically different.

The testimony of the doctors who recommended surgery justified not an adjudication of neglect but rather a reaffirmation of parental autonomy. The doctors admitted that "the disease poses no immediate threat to [Kevin's] life nor has it yet seriously affected his general health" and that surgery was very risky and offered no cure. Further, the doctors found in the central nervous system no brain or spinal cord involvement and concluded that delay until his majority would decrease, not increase, the risk. Yet the court replied:

> [T]o postpone the surgery merely to allow the boy to become of age so that he may make the decision himself as suggested by the surgeon and urged by both counsel for the mother and the Law Guardian . . . totally ignores the developmental and psychological factors stemming from his deformity which the Court deems to be of the utmost importance in any consideration of the boy's future welfare and begs the whole question.[18]

Without regard to the relationship of Kevin's well-being to the integrity of his family, the court added: " 'Neither by statute nor decision is the child's consent necessary or material, and we should not permit his refusal to agree, his failure to co-operate, to ruin his life and any chance for a normal, happy existence.' " [14]

— Judge Elwyn, in the role of prophet, psychological expert, risk-taker, and all-knowing parent, described but ignored a powerful reason for concluding that state authority should not supervene parental judgments about the rightness for their child of a recommended medical treatment when death is not an issue. He wrote:

> It is conceded that 'there are important considerations both ways' and that the views expressed by the dissenting Judges in *Seiferth* have not been universally accepted. Moreover, it must also be humbly acknowledged that under the circumstances of this case 'one cannot be certain of being right'. . . . Nevertheless, a decision must be made, and so, after much deliberation, I am persuaded that if this court is to meet its responsibilities to this boy it can neither shift the responsibility for the ultimate decision onto his shoulders nor can it permit his mother . . . to stand in the way of attaining through corrective surgery whatever chance he may have for a normal, happy existence, which . . . is difficult of attainment under the most propitious circumstances, but will unquestionably be impossible if the disfigurement is not corrected. [15]

Genuine humility would not have allowed a judge to believe that he, rather than Kevin's mother, was best qualified to determine the meaning of "a normal and happy existence" for her son. In Kevin's eyes, either might be proven "wrong" retrospectively. But nothing can qualify a judge to make that prediction with equal or greater accuracy than a parent. Nor is any judge prepared or obligated, as are parents, to assume day-to-day responsibility for giving their Kevins the personal care they may require. Judges cannot be substitute parents and courts cannot be substitute families.

In another case, a New York court refused to find 14-year-old Martin Seiferth a neglected child, even though his father would not compel him to undergo the surgery recommended for repair of a cleft palate and harelip.[16] Martin's father would have consented to surgery despite his belief that it was undesirable—had Martin been willing. Despite medical evidence far less equivocal than that in Kevin's case, the court refused to be trapped by the rescue fantasies of health department doctors or by strong societal prejudices which it was being asked to reinforce in an effort to "save" the child from himself and his parents. The court refused to order surgery, not because it thought it lacked authority, but because it thought Martin's reluctance to have the surgery foretold an unwillingness to participate in the therapy following the operations. Thus it was unwilling, unlike Judge Elwyn, to substitute its or a state agency's value preferences for those of the responsible parents.

If Martin Seiferth had later chosen to undergo the recommended surgery as an adult, his decision would have no bearing on the argument. The court should not have had discretion to do other than what it did at the time—protect him and his parents from state intrusion. In fact, even as an adult Martin chose not to have the surgery. "After attending one of the vocational high schools in the city, where he learned the trade of upholsterer and was elected president of the Student Council, he set up in business on his own and is, despite his disfigurement, active and successful." [17] Nevertheless, the county health department that originated the case reacted a decade later as if experience offered no lessons about the need to respect family integrity:

> [He] had graduated from . . . High School . . . at the head of the graduating class. It was his intention then to become an interior decorator. I have no *personal* comments to make except that . . . the operation should have been performed in order to give this young man a fuller opportunity for the development of his talents.[18]

WHEN DEATH IS AN ISSUE UNLESS A HEALTHY SIBLING PROVIDES A TRANSPLANT

The application of this ground for intervention is further clarified by considering what authority, if any, the state would have to investigate and review the deliberations of parents who must decide whether to let one of their children die or whether to attempt to supply a lifesaving organ for transplant by consenting to "unnecessary" surgery on one of their healthy children.

Under this ground the state would not be empowered to intrude.

In *Hart* v. *Brown*,[19] however, though the court eventually upheld the choice of the parents, it asserted the state's authority to review and supervene their judgment. The doctors had advised Mr. and Mrs. Hart that the only real prospect for saving their 8-year-old daughter Katheleen's life from a deadly kidney malfunction was to transplant a kidney from Margaret, her healthy twin sister. The doctors recommended and the Hart parents consented to the "unnecessary" surgery on Margaret to provide Katheleen with an opportunity to pursue a relatively normal life. But the hospital administration and the doctors refused to accept parental consent without a court review.[20] They acted out of a concern for their livelihood, not for the lives or wellbeing of Margaret or of Katheleen. Understandably, they feared becoming liable for money damages because the law might not accept the parents' consent as a defense to possible assault or malpractice suits.[21]

The Harts were thus forced to turn to the state to establish either their authority to decide or the rightness of their decision. They initiated proceedings before Judge Testo which intruded massively on the privacy of the family and set a dangerous precedent for state interference with parental autonomy. There was no *probable cause* to suspect that the parents might be exploiting either of their children. The court upheld the parental choice, though not their autonomy to decide.

Although Judge Testo's decision avoided tragic consequences for the Harts, he did set a precedent for unwarranted and undesirable intervention by the state. He held:

> To prohibit the natural parents and the guard-
> ians ad litem of the minor children the right to
> give their consent under these circumstances,
> *where there is supervision by this court and other
> persons in examining their judgment,* would be
> most unjust, inequitable and injudicious. There-
> fore, natural parents of a minor should have the
> right to give their consent to an isograft kidney
> transplantation procedure *when their motiva-
> tion and reasoning are favorably reviewed by a
> community representation which includes a court
> of equity.*[22]

Had the Hart parents refused to consent to Margaret's surgery and the transplant of her kidney to Katheleen, equally unwarranted proceedings might have been brought to establish their neglect in order to obtain court authority to impose the doctors' recommendation. Because of their special training, doctors can make diagnoses and prognoses; doctors can also indicate the probable consequences for a Margaret or a Katheleen of pursuing one course or another. But in the absence of a societal consensus, nothing in their training, or for that matter in the training of judges, qualifies them to impose upon others their preferred value choices about what is good or right for such children or their families. The critical fallacy is to assume, as Judge Testo did in his declaratory judgment—as the legislature does in its laws of neglect and abuse—that the

training and offices of doctors, legislators, and judges
endow them not just with the authority but also with
the capacity to determine what risks to take for someone else's child, in circumstances where no answer is
right or wrong.

We recognize that some will object to and be
uneasy about the substantial limits this ground would
place upon the power of the state to supervene parental
decisions about health care for their children. But the
absence of a substantial societal consensus about the
legitimacy of state intrusion concerning these matters
is the best evidence for holding in check the use of state
power to impose highly personal values on those who
do not share them. Further, the parameters set by the
criteria of normal healthy growth toward adulthood or
a life worth living, of the life-or-death choice, and of
proven medical procedures have a built-in flexibility
which can respond both to new findings in medicine
and to a new and changing consensus in society. Finally,
this ground's limits must be considered in the context
of the scope of the ground, discussed in Chapter 5,
which concerns serious bodily injury as well as the repeated failure of parents to prevent their child from
suffering such harm.

Chapter 7

The Child's Need for Legal Assistance

*A REQUEST BY PARENTS WHO ARE UNABLE
TO OBTAIN LEGAL ASSISTANCE FOR THEIR
CHILDREN, AN ADJUDICATION OF ANY
GROUND FOR MODIFYING OR TERMINATING
PARENT-CHILD RELATIONSHIPS, OR AN
EMERGENCY PLACEMENT PENDING
ADJUDICATION SHOULD BE A GROUND
FOR THE APPOINTMENT OF A LAWYER TO
REPRESENT THE CHILD*

This ground for intervention is designed to assure legal
assistance in the child placement process for the child
whose parents have been disqualified as the exclusive
representatives of his interests and for the child whose
parents believe he needs a lawyer and are unable to
obtain one for him. Under this ground the state could
(1) *provide* legal counsel for children only upon the
request of parents who cannot afford or obtain such
assistance; and (2) *impose* such services without parental consent only (a) *after* an adjudication that estab-

111

lishes a ground for modifying or terminating a parent-child relationship, or (b) *before* such an adjudication, during an emergency placement when a child is temporarily placed under state care and outside parental control. This formulation accords with our preference for the least intrusive invocation and adjudication.

This ground recognizes that an integral part of the autonomy of parents is their authority and presumed capacity to determine whether and how to meet the legal care needs for their child—just as they do with regard to his medical care needs. It acknowledges that parents, or those they select, are the exclusive representatives of their children before the law, even though the needs of individual family members differ.

The appointment of counsel for a child without regard to the wishes of parents is a drastic alteration of the parent-child relationship. Indeed, it is in effect a disposition by the state. It intrudes upon the integrity of the family and strains the psychological bonds that hold it together. Therefore it cannot take place until the presumption of parental autonomy has been overcome—until the protective insulation that parents give children from the law has been broken by the establishment at adjudication of a ground for intervention.

The imposition of counsel by the state is, however, a disposition for a limited purpose and a limited time. Such counsel are to act as lawyers, not as parents. They are to represent a child's legal needs by gathering and providing the court with information that it requires in order to determine the least detrimental placement. But like doctors ordered to provide medical assistance, lawyers are not to be perceived as substitutes for nurturing parents. Nurture is to be provided by the caretaking adults—either parents (natural, adoptive, or longtime foster) or state agencies—who are to retain physical custody of the child pending a final disposition.

The duration of the appointment of such counsel is limited to the period of suspended judgment between adjudication and final disposition or, in the event of emergency placements, to the period between invocation and final disposition.* Only during those periods does a child require party status and representation by a lawyer who is independent of both child care agencies and parents. Such children must have their interests represented and protected by counsel until the least detrimental alternative placement has been arranged. At that point, whoever is designated as parents should be allowed to assume or resume full responsibility for all matters concerned with their child's care, including whether and for what purposes the child should have a lawyer and who that lawyer should be.

Under this ground for intervention, parents are entitled to arrange for counsel on behalf of their child at any point in the child placement process. But contrary to current practice, there would be no justification for the imposition of a lawyer for a child at invocation in what are now called neglect, abuse, or delinquency proceedings, when no more than a *charge* of one of the grounds for modification or termination is made. To appoint counsel for a child without parental consent is to deny both parents and child due process. It deprives parents of their right to represent their child through

* Concerning suspended judgments, see Chapter 2, p. 23.

their own counsel,* with counsel they choose for their
child, or even without counsel. It is to presume on
the basis of an unproven charge—an unestablished
ground—that parents are incompetent to represent the
interests of their family and consequently the interests
of their child. It is also to deprive the child of his right
to be represented by his parents before the law.† On
the other hand, not to appoint legal counsel for a child
after adjudication establishes a ground for modifying
or terminating his relationship to his parents, and *before disposition,* would be to expose him, uninsulated
by an adult, to the state's authority.[2] At that point, a
child in most cases [3] will require a legal representative
who will assure that the process of disposition and the
placement itself will make his interests paramount and
provide him with the least detrimental alternative.

Likewise, a child requires representation by counsel during emergencies when there is good reason to
believe that he has no adult caretaker or that he is in

---

* Usually the same lawyer can represent both parent and
child without conflict because the *family's* interests are being represented. However, in delinquency proceedings, especially those involving offenses in which parents are charged in a criminal proceeding with being participants, there may be conflicts of interest.
In neglect proceedings, one must not assume that there is a conflict
of interest between parent and child until after an adjudication of
neglect.

† We now find unsatisfactory para. 30.4 of the Hampstead-
Haven Code: "Whenever an intervenor seeks to alter a child's
placement the child shall be made a party to the dispute. The child
shall be represented by independent counsel." [1] We would amend it
to read: "Whenever *a ground has been established for modifying
a parent-child relationship,* a child shall be made a party to the
dispute. . . ."

imminent danger of serious bodily injury. He is then taken from his parents pending adjudication and placed in the care of a state agency until final disposition. Such emergency decisions telescope invocation, adjudication, and disposition into a single transaction and not only place the child outside of the care and control of his parents but also temporarily disqualify them to represent his immediate interests. To assure that the state provides the child in an emergency with adequate care until the placement process has run its course, it is necessary that he be represented by a lawyer.

In divorce and separation proceedings, the imposition of counsel under this ground is justified only if the parents are unable to decide custody on their own—that is, if they ask the court to decide. By failing to agree on a disposition, separating parents waive their claim to parental autonomy and thereby their right to be the exclusive representatives of their child's interests. The child then requires representation independent of his parents' to assure that his interests are treated as paramount in determining who shall have custody.

Whatever the nature of the proceeding, the continuity guideline generally requires that the same lawyer represent all of the children within a family. These children share a community of interests in maintaining their ties with one another. There may be exceptional cases when this presumption should be overcome and individual children within the same family should be accorded separate representation. Once a final disposition is made, of course, each child is presumed to have at least one autonomous parent who is responsible for sheltering him from direct contact with the law and for generally representing his interests as a member of the family. That parent becomes responsible for determining the child's legal care needs, including the decision not to retain counsel.

By failing to give explicit recognition to the interests that children have as individuals or as a class * in the autonomy of their parents to make decisions about their legal care needs, legislators, judges, and commentators (including ourselves) [6] have failed to

* In a legal action involving the common claims of many children as a class—foster children, for example—courts should assure that the children comprising the class are represented by counsel selected by or with the consent of their parents or appoint counsel for them if their parents or longtime caretakers have been disqualified as their sole representatives.[4] It is necessary to recognize two possibly conflicting roles for counsel representing children as a class. The goals of such counsel may be more legislative than remedial. For example, counsel may attempt to establish—in the public interest—a constitutional right to a certain procedure or the unconstitutionality of a particular procedure, in order to assure a fairer administration of the child care system in the future. But that role may require counsel to ignore or even sacrifice the particular needs of individual members of the class. In such cases, lawyers for the class must clarify for themselves the distinction between establishing what and whose *rights* may have been violated, and what *remedy* is most appropriate for the individual members of the class. New or restored placements for the particular children in the class whose rights or whose parents' rights may have been violated should not necessarily be the remedy. For example, children taken away from their parents by unconstitutional procedures would not be well served if they are returned to long-absent parents and separated from their longtime caretakers. Particular children in the class must not be sacrificed for the principle that counsel for a class of children may be trying to establish. Indeed, it may be that children within a class should have separate counsel if the remedy involves the possibility of new placements.[5]

clarify how the role of the lawyer for a child client may differ from his role in relation to adult clients. Possibly because of its relatively recent origins, the idea of legal care for children as persons in their own right has often been perceived as an unmitigated good. Although unwanted medical care is recognized to be potentially harmful, the imposition of legal care for a child is presumed to be benign, and thus not something requiring parental consent.

Resistance to the idea of independent counsel rightly rested on the presumption in law that a child's parents (or the protective agency responsible for him, or even the courts) were best and most adequately suited to represent and safeguard his interests. Such opposition to separate counsel for a child was flawed, however, because it failed to recognize that the presumption of parental autonomy can be overcome. It further failed to recognize that state policies and practices that are intended to serve the best interests of children cannot always be relied upon to assure the best interests of a particular child. Some proponents of legal representation for children exposed these flaws only to lose sight of the presumption of parental autonomy altogether. They succeeded in having courts empowered to impose counsel not only at adjudication but also at invocation and even to extend such appointments beyond the disposition stage. These groundless violations of family integrity have led to confusion about the nature of the imposed counsel's relationship and responsibility to a child client. The preliminary but obscured question that must be confronted in order to clarify that relationship is:

Who, if anyone, is to assume responsibility for deciding to engage, to instruct, and to dismiss a lawyer for a child whose parents have been disqualified to make these decisions?

In order to answer this question concerning state-imposed counsel, we first examine the nature of the relationships of "parent-imposed" counsel to both child and parents.

IMPLICATIONS

TO WHOM IS COUNSEL FOR A CHILD RESPONSIBLE?

a. *When Parents Engage or Request Counsel*

Charlie, a 10-year-old who tried to hire his own lawyer, helped us clarify for ourselves what it means to have a child as a "client." Charlie telephoned us long distance and asked:

Are you the people, the lawyers, who represent kids? I want you to help me. My parents are divorced. They're always fighting over visits with me and my sister Irene.

We told Charlie that before we could give him an answer we would have to know if the judge had already decided which of his parents had custody. He replied:

My mother has custody. But why do you have to know that? I'm asking you to represent me.

We replied that since his mother had custody, it was her responsibility to decide whether Charlie needed the assistance of a lawyer and that, if she decided that he needed one, she would choose the lawyer she wanted for him. We would not represent him without his mother's consent, we said. He responded:

> I don't understand that. My mother may not want me to have a lawyer, and I want one.

We replied that what he wanted might not be what his mother thought best for him and that one of the reasons for having parents is to have someone to make such decisions for their children. We explained that just as parents decided when to seek the services of a doctor or a dentist, it was also their responsibility to decide whether to consult a lawyer. In Charlie's case we would not agree to his request unless his mother thought that he needed a lawyer and engaged us on his behalf. We asked Charlie if his mother knew about the phone call. He replied:

> Yes, she's right here. She'd like to talk to you.

Charlie's mother understood our position. She said that she wanted us to counsel Charlie and Irene:

> I want the children to visit their father. I encourage them to do so. But Charlie has good reasons for not wanting to observe the schedule established by the court. More important, my lawyer and their father's lawyer confuse the children with different explanations for why they must obey the court. Charlie keeps asking: "Why

do we have to obey the court if daddy doesn't?
He can cancel visits." I want you to clarify for
Charlie and Irene what is going on.

We accepted her request on the understanding that we
would counsel her children, advise her as to their
needs—always making clear to them that she, as their
custodial parent, had final say both with regard to accepting our advice and to our continuing to provide
representation. What we sought to accomplish on behalf of the two children in our negotiations with counsel
for each of the parents and in testimony before the
court was done with the consent and at the request of
Mrs. Martin. We were guided by her wishes—by what
she as primary parent ultimately determined would
best serve the interests of her family.

One event occurred almost a year later which
allowed us to define further our relationship to our
clients. Toward the close of a long winter holiday visit
with his father (which his mother insisted he make),
Charlie called us long distance and said:

Call mother. I don't want to go home. Tell her
I'm staying with daddy.

We told Charlie that we would try to reach his mother,
that we would tell her about the call, but that since she
expected him to be home the next day, he had to return unless she called to say it was "o.k." to stay.
Charlie, obviously annoyed, said:

> You call her, tell her I'm not coming back. You're
> my lawyers. You tell her what I want and get
> her to do it.

Again we reminded Charlie that what his mother decided he needed was not always the same as what he
wanted and that we would not tell his mother what
she was to do. Despite our consistent efforts to respect
his mother's autonomy as a parent, Charlie obviously
thought that it was worth trying to maneuver us into
a position which would undermine his mother's authority. When this failed, he returned home as scheduled.

What Charlie mistakenly sought to arrogate to
himself was the status of an adult. He tried to choose
his counsel, instruct them with regard to his wishes and
intentions, and with their help fight his case with his
parents. None of this is open to the child unless, of
course, his parents instruct counsel to abide by their
child's wishes. A child may have his wishes taken into
consideration by his parents. But, like Charlie, every
child before the law finds himself in the position where
the adults "know best" what is good for him and decide
that with or without regard to his wishes.[7]

b. *When the Court Imposes Counsel*

Once the court has imposed counsel for a child,
from whom is counsel to receive his instructions? The
answer is that counsel must turn to the court and to
the legislature for the guidance he would normally receive from autonomous parents who engage him to represent their children.

Counsel imposed by the court may look to the parents and the child as sources of information, but not for instructions. The parents have voluntarily abdicated or have been disqualified as the exclusive representatives of their child's interests. Counsel cannot turn directly to the children whom he represents for his instructions. Children are by definition persons in need of adult caretakers who determine what is best for them. Nor may counsel seek to have his personal child-rearing preferences imposed upon his "client" without regard to the state's notion of what is best for children.

Like an autonomous parent, the court must advise counsel. But it must advise as the child placement statutes direct. For example, statutes might require that placements maximize the opportunity for continuity of current or, if necessary, new relationships. And counsel might be required with regard to both process and substance to press the court to take into account the child's sense of time and the limitation of experts to make long-range predictions and of courts to monitor parent-child relationships. The court, like an autonomous parent, may find unconvincing and reject evidence or recommendations of counsel for the child.* And like a parent, the court may dismiss counsel who fail to perform their duties.[8] However, unlike the autonomous parent, the court may not dismiss counsel without good cause. It does not have the final say. Counsel is empowered to appeal decisions that he believes conflict with statutory standards.

* Child care agencies and disqualified parents remain parties to such proceedings. Their counsel represent what they believe to be the child's best interests.

Finally, counsel appointed before adjudication for a child in an emergency placement will be responsible for monitoring the child's custody in order to assure that the state does provide the nurturing care decreed by the court.

Thus, the court temporarily assumes the authority of a parent to determine the legal care needs of a child during that stage of the child placement process when it must decide who is to be the parent. In a disposition proceeding, unlike other legal proceedings, the court knows prior to the introduction of any evidence—prior to a hearing—which party it will favor. The court is obligated by statute, except in some delinquency proceedings, to make the child's interests paramount—to favor the child. Counsel for the child knows his client is supposed to win. That is another way of coming to understand why the court can generally be relied upon to serve as the parent substitute in relation to counsel. In order to compensate for the loss of full parental insulation, in order to protect the now-exposed child from judicial and child care agency policies and practices which might ignore or conflict with a particular child's interests, the court is obligated to appoint "independent" counsel to represent the child pending disposition.

Once disposition is final, once the court determines who is to be the child's caretaker, the role of both the court and the child's counsel has come to an end. The child is restored to and is under the care and direction of a parental authority. In designating a custodial parent, the court expresses the state's confidence that this particular adult has the greatest capacity among those available to fulfill the child's needs, including his need to be protected from and represented before the law. To do otherwise—to impose continuing legal counsel for the child as a condition of a disposition—is to undermine that confidence. It is to threaten rather than promote family integrity.

Yet this is what the Connecticut Superior Court did in *G*. v. *G*. Richard, age 13, was represented by counsel appointed at the request of the custodial parent who wanted to prevent the noncustodial parent from resuming visits which the court had suspended. The battle over visitation had been in and out of court for more than 9 years. Accepting the arguments made both by counsel for the custodial parent and by counsel for the child, the court denied the request for visits. But it ordered what this ground prohibits—that the lawyer continue to represent Richard after disposition. The court observed:

> The attorney for the minor child has consented to remain as counsel of record. The child should feel free to consult with his attorney at any time pertaining to matters regarding his custody.
>
> Of course without further order of this court and with the consent of the plaintiff-mother [the custodial parent] *and* the consent of the minor child through his attorney, visitation may be resumed under appropriate arrangements. . . .
>
> It should be made clear that consent of both the plaintiff-mother and the minor child or an order

of this court must be obtained before there can be a resumption of visitation.[9]

By interposing an attorney between Richard and his mother, the court undermined their opportunity to relate directly to one another. The court obtained only the consent of the attorney, not of the custodial parent, for extending the appointment of Richard's counsel. Richard was thus deprived of a parent who had authority to grant or deny his wishes, to determine his needs, and to represent his interests—even to decide whether he required legal assistance. His mother could not, for example, make him visit his father or grant him permission to do so. She would first have to obtain the concurrence of Richard's counsel or permission from the court to overcome counsel's objection. And were counsel to decide over the mother's objection that visits should be resumed, he could seek judicial supervention of her judgment.

By imposing conditions of this kind, a court places itself and counsel between parent and child. It subverts rather than safeguards the child's critical need for an autonomous parent. Currently, the only continuity Richard and his parents can anticipate is the continuity of state intrusion. Occasions for court orders as intrusive and as divisive as that in *G*. v. *G*. would be minimized, if not eliminated, in a child placement system which observed the least-detrimental-alternative standard and made all placements permanent, unconditional, and final (except for emergency, institutional, and truly temporary foster care).[10] But whatever the state's policy with regard to visits and other conditions of custody, our ground precludes appointment of counsel for the child after disposition without the consent of the custodial parent.

SHOULD ADOLESCENTS BE EMANCIPATED TO DETERMINE THEIR OWN LEGAL CARE NEEDS?

Should some adolescents be given the authority, free of adult control, to engage, direct, and dismiss their own lawyers? Like adults, such children would be presumed both competent and free to determine their own placement needs and to arrange to meet them. Put another way, are there circumstances which should justify the state's presuming that a child is as competent as an adult and thus entitled to be free of the care and control of his parents or some other adult authority?

Any affirmative answer to this question which would qualify a minor as an adult must provide a standard of emancipation which is as impersonal and as nonjudgmental as is chronological age for establishing adult status. To require objective criteria for emancipation is not to take a simplistic view of children. Rather it is to recognize (a) the difference between a child and an adult; (b) how varied and complex are parents and children and their ties to each other; and (c) how impersonal and thus how inadequate courts are for judging the capacity of an individual child for making and "benefiting" from his decision as to who should be his "parent" or that he does not need a "parent." [11]

For the emancipation to be real, all children in a specific category—for example, children institutionalized at their parents' request, children who are pregnant, or children over 14 years of age—would have to be deemed qualified to refuse as well as to accept the service and advice of counsel. Emancipation would be a fiction if it covered only those children in such categories who "choose" to accept counsel or who are found to be "mature enough" on a case-by-case basis to make decisions for themselves. That would only transfer the prerogative and responsibility to decide from the parent, who has not been disqualified, to the judge—not to the child.

A genuine emancipation statute which would meet the fair-warning and power-restraint requirements of a ground for terminating parent-child relationships could be drafted. For example, all children age 13 could be freed of both parental and court control in determining their legal care needs. But we do not recommend any such provisions because we do not believe that there are or can be circumstances which justify emancipating children to meet their own legal care needs in the child placement process. Indeed, it is the purpose of the process to secure or restore for every child an uninterrupted opportunity to be represented by "parents." Because they are children, they require representation by parents or by some other adult upon the disqualification of their parents. They are persons in their own right but are not adults in their own right. Children by definition cannot be free of an adult's control in determining either their need for legal assistance or what lawyers must seek on their behalf in the process of their placement.

This ground recognizes only one situation in

which a child may be treated as an adult with the authority to engage [12] a lawyer or to instruct him as to what course to pursue. That is when his parents delegate such authority to him. Otherwise, whether engaged by autonomous parents or by a judge, counsel for a child may be advised to take into account the child's wishes in representing his interests.[13] But such a child, because he is a child and not an adult, is without authority to engage or dismiss his counsel.

The 1967 decision of the United States Supreme Court in *In re Gault* [14] extended the right to counsel to children charged with delinquency, but it did not emancipate them for legal service purposes. This decision is often misconstrued to mean that the parents of such children are not to be relied upon to protect their infant's interests. That erroneous reading is used to disqualify parents, without process, as the representatives of their child and to deprive children, without process, of their parents' representation.[15]

Gault means that a child in a juvenile delinquency proceeding will not be deprived of the right to legal representation because his parents are financially unable to afford counsel. Indeed, the parents of young Gault initiated the lawsuit in order to assure that they were not denied the right as his representatives—as insulating adults—to provide their son with the legal representation they believed he needed and to which he was entitled. It was a right that they were unwilling to waive.[16] The *Gault* Court held that "the child *and his parents* must be notified of the child's right to be represented by counsel retained by them, or if they are unable to afford counsel, that counsel will be appointed to represent the child." [17]

Looked at more broadly, *Gault* was an attempt to prevent juvenile "justice" from usurping parental functions. The decision grew out of the Court's recognition that the juvenile delinquency system had failed to meet the special and individual needs of children caught up in an otherwise heartless, nonrehabilitative system of criminal law. By the time young Gault entered the juvenile system, it had become in many ways as punitive and "inhumane" as its adult counterpart. In fact, it had become even more "inhumane," for adults are presumed capable of protecting their own interests.

Rather than extend the authority of juvenile court judges or other state agents to act as parent to the child, *Gault* reaffirms the right of a child to have his own parents make decisions about what he needs. There is no hint in *Gault,* and it would run contrary to its tenor, that an attorney could independently represent the child over the parents' objection and prior to their disqualification as the exclusive representatives of his interests. Protection of the family, protection of the child from the state—not from his parents—is central to the holding in *Gault* and indeed to what we propose as criteria in this ground for the appointment and function of counsel for children.

Part Three

The Agonizing Dilemma

Chapter 8

Too Early, Too Late,
Too Much, or Too Little

In writing and rewriting this book we have been constantly aware of a pressure within us to use the legal system to meet every situation in which a child needs help. We had to remind ourselves that neither law, nor medicine, nor science has magical powers and that there is no societal consensus about what is "best" or even "good" for all children. More than that, we had to address the tension between the fear of encouraging the state to violate a family's integrity before intervention is justified and the fear of inhibiting the state until it may be too late to protect the child whose well-being is threatened.

We respect parental rights based on the fact of reproduction. We see the biological connection as a powerful motivating force for most parents to provide their children with continuous affectionate and responsible care. But we recognize that a child's attachments and healthy development do not rest on biology alone. They ultimately depend on the adult caretaker's reciprocal affection in day-to-day care and attention to the child's needs. Moreover, society's belief in the blood tie exists side by side with a growing apprehension about the general deterioration and dissolution of family life and of the plight of many children whose parents fail to discharge their responsibilities. Thus, moves *against* and *for* state-sponsored intrusion upon parent autonomy vie with each other in a world where parental authority is frequently abusive, harmful, and detrimental to the child; where the child's essential tie to his parents ceases to be beneficial in families torn internally by parental violence or indifference; where state interference, under the cloak of the child's best interests, is sometimes no more than the wielding of power by authoritarian figures who try to impose their own standards on differently minded parents; and where well-intentioned rescue attempts may serve merely to destroy remaining family attachments while failing to provide children with the necessary substitutes.

Under existing grounds for intervention, the courts and social service agencies can be held to do too little, and often too late, to ensure the next generation's growth toward healthy adulthood. Frequently, battered infants are returned to the same parents who have harmed them and who may do so again. Attempts on a child's life are not considered sufficient to bar the same parents from later access to their victim, regardless of that child's fear of repetition and complete lack of trust. A mother's abandonment of a helpless infant, leaving him to starve in a deserted flat, does not automatically terminate her right to delay or prevent his adoption or to visit him in his new "place of safety" and interfere with his caretaking.

By contrast, under existing grounds for intervention state authorities may be held to do too much, or to do it too early on insufficient evidence. Conditions deemed chaotic and unsanitary in a parental home may prompt authorities to move in and disperse a family before inquiring into the members' ties to each other and without recognizing the distress caused by their disruption. Courts may interpose legal representatives between child and custodial mother instead of returning a child as speedily as possible to the care of an autonomous parent. In matters of health, a judge may deem it his duty to uphold his own medical preference without regard to that of the parents. The duty to report cases of suspected child battering, instead of being the benefit intended, has frequently prevented parents from seeking medical help for the injured child; has broken their confidential relationship with doctors and nurses; and has exposed innocent parents to harrassment and distress in cases where the suspicion of intentional harm proved unjustified.

Finally, the combination of too much and too little official action is evident in the area of foster placement, quite apart from failures due to the fostering adults themselves. By failing to keep families together, by failing to restrict foster care to children who have a real chance of being returned to their absent parents in a "short time," and by failing to regard longtime foster parents as autonomous, the authorities prevent feelings of security from developing in either child or adult. By moving children from placement to placement in the interests of absent parents, the state interferes with the attachments that are essential for an individual's growth. By returning children in familiar foster homes to estranged biological parents, the state disregards and disrupts psychological bonds, causing distress to the child and harming his development.

This is the muddled and badly defined situation that we have sought to address. In dividing the child placement decision-making process into the three stages of invocation, adjudication, and disposition; in requiring that the definition of each ground for intervention meet the standards of fair warning and power restriction; and in recognizing that no human system of regulation can be perfect, we have sought to hold in check our rescue fantasies and to ensure that the state be authorized to intervene if and only if it provides the child in jeopardy with a less detrimental alternative. We had to acknowledge that safeguarding the well-being of every child has to be frustrated by the limits of our knowledge, by the limitations of all those who seek to help, and consequently by society's need to restrict coercive intervention to "objectively" definable grounds. This has meant, as does the drawing of any line, leaving out some children whom we would wish to protect. To do otherwise would have required—because of the inherent ambiguity of words alone—the inclusion of many children and families that it would be arbitrary, if not harmful, to cover. Overinclusion would have meant leaving agents of the state with too much discretion.

Because harm is inherent in every violation of family integrity, we decided to err on the side of non-intrusiveness. In a continuing reexamination of our preferences for minimum state intervention on *de facto* family relationships and for making the child's interests paramount, we sought always to place ourselves in the position of children of different ages, of different developmental phases, and of different backgrounds. We established the correlative principles of least intrusive invocation, least intrusive adjudication, and least intrusive disposition. These principles are to be applied always in relation to ongoing, not necessarily *de jure,* family units. From the child's vantage point as a member of a family, we sought always to restrict coercive intervention to actual and threatened harm about which there is a consensus and about which there is a reasonable expectation that intrusion will be more beneficial than injurious to the child. In this way we sought to confront our fear of the state doing too little or too much, too early or too late.

In our search for a reasonably just law for children we have been mindful of Grant Gilmore's observation:

> Law reflects but in no sense determines the moral worth of a society. A reasonably just society will reflect its values in a reasonably just law. The better the society, the less law there will be. In Heaven there will be no law and the lion will lie down with the lamb. An unjust society will reflect its values in an unjust law. The worse the society, the more law there will be. In Hell there will be nothing but law, and due process will be meticulously observed.[1]

Were we living in a better society, there would be no need for this book. But there is a need to try to contribute even in a small way to making our world a little less unperfect for our children.[2] Thus, by applying the guidelines of *Beyond the Best Interests of the Child*[3] and by defining in objective, precise terms the justifications for state intrusion into family relationships, we hope we have provided a basis for a more balanced view of the problem and for a more just regulation of decisions and procedures that will assure as many children as possible a permanent membership in a caring family.

Part Four

❖

Appendices

Appendix I

On Children Killed by Their Parents

INTRODUCTION

There is no lack of evidence that children can suffer severe mutilation and death at the hands of their parents, or that state interference with the psychological parent-child relationship can have disastrous consequences. There are too many cases which somehow slip through the net of the manifold dispositions and elaborate regulations which are devised for the protection of children. To cite only a few:

In Tennessee, Melisha Gibson, a girl of 4, died in 1976, after being forced by her stepfather to march around the house for 3 days and after a prolonged beating when she begged to stop. Both her stepfather and her biological mother were charged with murder. Angered citizens collected money for the child's funeral and 250 people from the neighborhood signed a petition demanding an investigation of why Melisha had been returned to parents who, 3 years earlier, had been convicted of abusing the child and had served a year's jail sentence for the offense.

In England, on 19 February, 1976, Karen Spencer, 2 months of age, "was admitted to hospital with injuries, including a fractured skull, inflicted by her mother. Karen remained in hospital until the end of March and during that time a care order was made, placing her in the care of the local authority, the Derbyshire County Council. On discharge from hospital Karen was placed with foster parents. She remained with them for twelve months, but was at home with her natural parents for visits most weekends and for longer periods at holiday times. The length of the visits gradually increased until at the end of March 1977 Karen was home on trial on a full-time basis. On 16 April 1977 she was again assaulted by her mother and sustained severe head injuries from which she died three days later."

In Colorado, in 1977, Jill, a 7-year-old girl, died of asphyxiation at the hands of her stepfather. Jill had been abused in 1976 and was removed by court order from her home for 6 months while her mother and stepfather received rehabilitative treatment. Soon after her return home, the school reported that the child had been abused again. The Assistant County Prosecutor called the welfare agency's actions into question since they "appeared to be more worried about keeping the family together than the safety of the child." He said that the stepfather had a history of abusing Jill for 2 years prior to her death and that he had abused his children of a previous marriage.

In Connecticut, in 1978, 14-month-old Angelo was killed by his 19-year-old mother. He was returned to her after his removal had been ordered a month earlier because she had hit and injured him when he cried too much and disobeyed her. The injuries consisted of a laceration under the left eye, a fracture of the right humerus, and numerous bruises over his chest and abdomen. The court returned

Angelo to his mother because it felt that she had benefited from taking a Red Cross course on parenting, and because the family promised to keep an eye on the situation. Three weeks after Angelo's return home, he was brought to the hospital emergency room, dead from multiple injuries inflicted by his mother.[1]

Meager as these accounts are, readers will recognize in them the eventualities against which one of our suggested grounds for state intervention with parent-child relationships is directed. Under the ground concerned with *serious bodily injury inflicted by parents,* the child would be removed immediately, parental rights would be terminated, and adoptive parents who wanted a child and could care for him on a permanent basis would be substituted for the original parents. The abusing parents might be encouraged to seek psychiatric and other appropriate assistance that would be useful in rehabilitating them, not for the battered child for whom this comes too late, but for those children they might have and care for in the future.

Neither the outcries of public indignation, nor trial by newspaper, nor emotionally tinged accusations against individuals are conducive to the atmosphere necessary for a sober appraisal and step-by-step examination of such events. In England, the death of a child, under circumstances similar to those under which Melisha, Karen, Jill, and Angelo died, actually led the Secretary of State for Social Services to appoint a Committee of Inquiry into the Care and Supervision Provided in Relation to Maria Colwell, a 7-year-old girl.[2] Maria had died at the hands of her stepfather in 1973. The inquiry into her death was held in public in

Brighton, Sussex. It lasted 41 days during which 70 witnesses were heard. While it caused considerable upset to the authorities and workers concerned, lessons learned from the inquiry triggered moves toward administrative changes and reformation of official and personal attitudes. According to one British social worker, practices in the Social Services can be divided into two eras: *before* and *after* Maria Colwell.[3]

If, in what follows, we quote in some detail from this Committee's Report, we do not do so for the purpose of reviving old, and by now perhaps partly forgotten, sensitivities; nor do we wish to join in a chorus of belated recriminations. We use the Report to check this child's life history against the grounds for state intervention set out in this book, and to examine whether and to what extent the application of these grounds might help to prevent, or at least limit, the future occurrence of tragedies of the same kind.

REPORT OF THE COMMITTEE OF INQUIRY INTO THE CARE AND SUPERVISION PROVIDED IN RELATION TO MARIA COLWELL (1974) [4]

CHAPTER 1
INTRODUCTION

1. We were appointed by Sir Keith Joseph, then Secretary of State for Social Services, on 17 July 1973 to inquire into and report upon the care and supervision provided by local authorities and other agencies in relation to Maria Colwell and the co-ordination between them.

5.   The inquiry was held in public in Brighton on 41 days [ending on] 7 December 1973. We heard oral evidence from 70 witnesses. . . .

CHAPTER 2
NARRATIVE*

10.   Maria Colwell was born on the 25th March 1965, so that when she died at the hands of her stepfather, William Kepple, on the night of the 6th/7th January 1973 she was eleven weeks short of her eighth birthday. She was the fifth and youngest child of her mother's first marriage and within weeks of her birth her father had left her mother at Conway Street, in Hove, and within a further few weeks he had died on the 22nd July 1965.

[11–14.   After the death of her husband, Maria's mother found it difficult to care for five young children. In August 1965, she took Maria to Mrs. Cooper, her sister-in-law, who agreed to look after her. In December 1965, the four older children were removed under a place of safety order and committed to the care of the East Sussex County Council.]

15.   Maria continued to live with Mr. and Mrs. Cooper, who moved meanwhile to Farm Road, Hove, until the 4th June 1966, when Mrs. Colwell removed her, as of course she was perfectly entitled to do since the arrangement under which the Coopers had looked after [Maria] since the previous August was an entirely private and voluntary one. This removal coincided apparently with her intention to set up house with her future husband Mr. Kepple. Of this first period during which the Coopers had the care of Maria it is enough to say that no word of criticism was voiced as to its

---

* Miss Stevenson dissents from this part of the narrative covering paragraphs 10–69.

sufficiency and that the contact maintained by Mrs. Colwell with her child was occasional and spasmodic but was in no way hindered or discouraged by the Coopers.

16. By the 11th June, only one week later, Mrs. Colwell had run into severe difficulties over housing and had either been forced, or chose, to part with Maria again, not returning her to the Coopers as might perhaps have been expected but leaving her with another woman in circumstances and conditions which Inspector Curran of the NSPCC [National Society for the Prevention of Cruelty to Children], who had knowledge of Maria's removal from the Coopers and also of the home in which Maria had been left, immediately recognised as requiring at once the obtaining of a place of safety order. Under the order Maria was returned by Inspector Curran to the Coopers as an interim measure. On the 17th August 1966 the Hove Juvenile Court made an order placing Maria in the care of the local authority, in this case also the East Sussex County Council (hereinafter called "East Sussex") who by now had all five of Mrs. Colwell's children in their care. . . . [A]fter careful consideration, East Sussex decided that the proper course was to board Maria out with the Coopers as foster parents, placing great reliance upon the satisfactory way the Coopers had looked after her for the past year and also the undesirability of yet another move if it could possibly be avoided. Accordingly, the Coopers, who were devoted to the child, being willing and anxious to continue to look after her, were approved as her foster parents by the Children's Committee on the 29th October 1966, and at the time it was clearly explained to them that the long-term plan was for Maria to return to her mother.

17. The point was made to us by East Sussex that the Coopers were not "ideal" foster parents. . . . In one respect we accept that they fell short of "ideal" in that one of the

qualities looked for in such foster parents is the willingness
actually to encourage a transfer back to the natural parent
when the time comes. This the Coopers, who were, after all,
part of Maria's wider natural family, understandably found it
impossible to do, although that is not to say that they ob-
structed the transfer. But the plain fact is that East Sussex
considered them suitable to foster Maria and saw no reason
to change that opinion as the years passed. . . .

19. After the Coopers were approved as foster parents they continued to look after Maria with the devotion
and care due to a child of their own and in those surroundings the little girl thrived and had a normal and satisfactory
upbringing. There was some evidence that Mrs. Cooper was
thought to be too doting in her attitude and might be said
to "spoil" her, but if this means no more than lavishing
affection on a child and seeking to provide whatever material advantages lie within one's station in life it might be
thought little harm can result. It was suggested—a little
faintly—that Maria was "spoilt" in the sense of going un-
rebuked or unpunished when this was merited but there was
no evidence of any substance upon which we could find she
was other than a nice, well-behaved little girl and one
wholly independent witness, Mrs. Hammer, who made her
acquaintance by accident over a period on Brighton Pier,
was impressed by her politeness and general behaviour. At a
later stage both her teachers were impressed by her man-
ners and behaviour which speaks well for her early upbringing. As regards contact with her mother, as is all too common in
such cases, there were allegations and counter-allegations as to
difficulties over access and this is not an issue upon which it
would have been either possible or profitable for us to pronounce. Suffice to say that Mr. Bennett and the successive
other social workers involved by no means took the view
that there was obstruction on the part of the Coopers who

themselves strenuously denied making access difficult, and we are certainly not prepared to find that they did, and access did in fact continue somewhat irregularly.

20.   The next event of significance was the proposal by the Coopers in July 1967 to have Maria christened, which was vetoed only two days before the ceremony by Mrs. Colwell on the ground that she had decided to become a Catholic and that when she married "Mr. Murphy"—as Mr. Kepple was then apparently known—she would have all her children baptised. This veto, and the manner of it, was hardly likely to endear her to the Cooper side of the family and may well have further stimulated the feud. Meanwhile, it is relevant to note that Mrs. Colwell had started her second family of children—those by Mr. Kepple—with the birth of a girl in November 1967 followed by a boy in December 1968 and another girl in November 1969, and also that by late 1967 or early 1968 Mrs. Cooper was anxious to adopt Maria if that were possible. This latter never became a live issue, however, owing to Mrs. Kepple's increasing pressure to have Maria back. The regular six monthly statutory reviews on Maria's progress and welfare continued to be entirely satisfactory.

22.   . . . Mrs. Colwell made plain to the social worker then in touch with her that while she would consent to her other children—all of whom were of course still in care—being brought up in the Church of England, she was determined that Maria should become a Catholic although she knew well that this would be bitterly resented by Mrs. Cooper, and the case notes record the social worker's opinion: "To me, this seems to be Pauline's (Mrs. Kepple's) way of maintaining some control over Maria. She resents her sister-in-law having this child."

23.   In June 1969 there were complaints of Mrs. Colwell and Mr. Kepple going out drinking and leaving the

children at night, and in March 1970 similar reports and the further allegation that Mrs. Colwell was the worse for drink were investigated by the social services duty officer, who thought that the children were unkempt and dirty and noticed that the eldest girl had a badly bruised right cheek with a scratch and a fading black eye, explained by Mrs. Colwell by the child falling against a table. The social worker thought it likely that Mrs. Colwell had hit the child in anger, although he acquitted her of drunkenness by the time he saw her.

25. In April 1970 two things of importance in the life of Maria occurred; first, she began to attend Middle Street Infants' School and secondly, there appeared to take over from the East Sussex social worker then in charge of her case, Mr. Bampfylde, a new social worker in the person of Miss Diana Lees, who was to continue to be responsible for Maria's welfare until the latter's death. This seems to be an appropriate point to quote from the last statutory six monthly report on Maria prepared by Mr. Bampfylde just before his handing over to Miss Lees and dated the 20th March 1970: "Maria relates closely to Mr. and Mrs. Cooper (whom she is still calling Mum and Dad). They respond well to her, Mrs. Cooper being perhaps rather over indulgent in some ways. Maria presents no problems, though is perhaps a little 'out of control,' very excitable. Maria is well settled with her aunt and uncle."

26. Miss Lees had excellent academic and professional qualifications with some previous experience in hospital social work. Until her arrival at East Sussex however she had no experience in local authority social work except during training. It is certainly relevant to a serious consideration of the facts of the last three years of Maria's life to realise that from when Miss Lees began to settle down in her first post that work load was steadily increased over the

period until by 1972 she was carrying an average burden of 60 to 70 cases of all sorts of which at any time there might be perhaps half a dozen involving children "at physical risk." This inevitably meant that a system of priorities for such a burden had to be exercised and as it was clear Miss Lees never at any time considered Maria to be at physical risk, it followed that absolute priority would not be devoted to her if other cases simultaneously demanded it. . . .

28.   On the next [routine] visit in July [1970] Mrs. Kepple informed Miss Lees of her hopes of an imminent move to a council house when she and Mr. Kepple would get married and that she would go to the Court to get Maria back when she was in a position to do so. As this was said in front of Maria, Miss Lees thought this an unsuitable conversation and managed to stop Mrs. Kepple "with difficulty". Later during the same visit when Maria was upset and crying for "mummy", Miss Lees noted that Mrs. Kepple very insensitively claimed that position in a tactless way. In view of later events it may well be that Maria's fears for her security and happy home at the Coopers were aroused then for the first time. Even very small children possess sometimes a remarkable acuity as to the implication of both situations and conversations which adults ignore at their peril and Maria was at this time over five years of age. Even if her unease did not date from this incident it clearly existed by October 1970 when Miss Lees attempted to take Maria from school to see her mother in the new council house at 119 Maresfield Road, Brighton to which the Kepples had moved that August. On that occasion Maria was so distressed that Miss Lees had to abandon the visit and she recorded also that Maria had been told by her mother that she would have her there to live with her. Mrs. Kepple by this time was adamant that she would have Maria to live with her as soon as possible, but Miss Lees observed that

never once had Mrs. Kepple said that this would be best for Maria. . . .

29. On the 27 November Maria spent the day quite happily at the Kepples and was thought to get on quite well with her eldest half-sister until the latter announced that Maria was going to sleep in the same room when she came to live with them whereupon Maria made obvious signs of wanting to leave.

30. On the 5 February 1971 Maria again went to her mother's when Miss Lees thought that Mr. Kepple seemed to show no understanding or concern for Maria and it seems fair to summarise his attitude both then and later in relation to Maria coming to join him and Mrs. Kepple as one of indifference in the sense that it was her concern and not his. . . . More visits took place on several occasions in March and April which seemed to go reasonably well and in March Mrs. Kepple was again consulting her solicitor about applying for revocation of the care order. By April she was anxious to know from Miss Lees whether she had to go to Court or whether Maria could go home on trial. . . .

36. [In response to Mrs. Kepple's urging, the East Sussex County caseworkers decided after one and half hours of discussion to increase Maria's contact with the Kepple family.] We were told that an accurate note of the discussion was taken, and because of its importance we set out below certain of the conclusions:

> "It would seem that whatever the decision was taken concerning Maria it would involve stress and trauma for her at some time. On balance it was felt that future plans should be directed towards her eventual return to her mother. . . . It is unlikely that the Coopers will be able to deal well with her feelings in adolescence concerning her natural parents [sic], and

it is possible that at this age she would herself decide
to return to her mother. It should be easier for her
to build relationships with the Kepple family and to
take her place within [it] at a younger age, particularly considering the good emotional grounding she
has received from the Coopers."

"It was seen that the best way to manage a
situation of this type would be for Maria's visits to
the Kepples to be gradually increased to include holi-
days, etc., and in this way to effect a gradual trans-
ferring of her roots from one family to the other. She
would then go home on trial whilst still remaining in
care and contact with the Coopers would gradually
diminish until revocation of the Order could be supported. However, this type of management would not
be possible in this case, because of the animosity between the Coopers and the Kepples, which is unlikely
to diminish. . . . On the other hand, her abrupt removal
from the people she considers her own family to a
household of which she knows relatively little would
be extremely damaging."

"It was felt that the best plan . . . was the
gradual changeover up to the point when the stress
for Maria appeared to be becoming too great, i.e.
contact with the Kepple family should be encouraged
and increased to give Maria the opportunity of
knowing them better before her sudden transfer to
them. With this in view, Mrs. Kepple should be encouraged to delay her application for revocation
and to go along with such a plan. If she insists on
making such an application she should be opposed
at this stage, but the long term plan of Maria's
return should be followed."

". . . Whatever action is taken one or other

of these people [the Coopers and Mrs. Kepple] will be hurt. But it was felt help could be given with this and Maria's interests must be considered as of paramount importance."

37. With much of this assessment and the conclusions reached we find ourselves in agreement. . . .

38. It is obvious not only that the most careful consideration was given to the situation as they saw it on this occasion by the East Sussex social workers but that they were determined to proceed with caution. There were, in our view, two specific matters which were absolutely basic to any correct decision as to Maria's future, whether that decision was merely a tentative and provisional one as on this occasion or a final decision made at some later date. These were (1) the question of whether it was really in Maria's best interests to be returned to her mother at all, and (2) the question of the true cause and depth of the trauma in Maria which it was envisaged would inevitably occur. To a great extent the answer to the second of those issues ought to be closely bound up with the answer to the first. Apart from that, no satisfactory answer to the first question could be given, either in April 1971 or at any time thereafter, without a full consideration of all the relevant circumstances. We think that East Sussex were precluded at that time, and continued to be so right up until the Juvenile Court hearing in November 1971, from reaching a correct decision as to whether Maria ought to return to her mother. This was because there was virtually a total lack of knowledge of at least one highly relevant factor, *i.e.* Mr. Kepple, and in addition there was a failure to interpret correctly the abundant available evidence in relation to another vital matter, *i.e.* Mrs. Kepple's physical and emotional condition.

42. It is clear that the social workers considering

the case in April did not consider themselves in a position to make an unfettered decision about Maria's future. They operated within a legal and social system in which when a child was taken into care the expectation was not that she would remain in care until the age of eighteen but that she would return to her own family when their circumstances had improved. It was put to us and we accept that there was a strong presumption that the magistrates would return a child to the parent once the parent's fitness was proved unless it could clearly be shown not to be in the best interests of the child. In Maria's case the social workers concerned took the view that Mrs. Kepple's application was likely to succeed within a short while given the improvement in her living conditions, her stable relationship with Mr. Kepple and her apparent ability to cope with the children living with her. With this in mind consideration was given to the harm which would result from a court decision to return Maria to her mother before Maria had had sufficient opportunity to get to know the Kepples. The social services department therefore was seeking in April 1971 to control the timing of a move. This view of the inevitability of Maria's return to her mother underlay much of the thinking in 1971 and profoundly affected the decisions taken and the management of the case.

46.   After the April case discussion the plan was put into effect. There were two short visits by Maria to see her mother after school during May. Nothing untoward was recorded as occurring. There was another visit on the 1st June. It was an all-day visit and during it Maria ran away to Mrs. Shirley, a sister of Mrs. Cooper living about half a mile away. When brought back by the latter to Mrs. Kepple, Maria had screamed and tried to run away again and Mrs. Kepple had slapped her.

47.   On the 6th and 12th June there were further day

visits but on the 16th Maria was taken by Mrs. Cooper to see Dr. Robinson because her nerves were bad, she bit her nails and she had difficulty in sleeping. The doctor gave her a nerve tonic and recommended that she need not see her mother if she did not want to. . . .

50. On the 14th July Maria resumed visits to her mother after a month's interval, going to her at first after school. She showed considerable resistance to the visit, sitting on the floor and screaming that she did not want to go. When she finally went Miss Lees thought she quite enjoyed herself and was fairly cheerful.

51. On the 16th July Maria spent her first night at her mother's but strenuously resisted going there. She eventually only went on condition Mr. Cooper travelled with her. She needed reassurance that she would return to the Coopers but the visit, according to Miss Lees, appeared to go fairly well. Later, Maria accused the Coopers on her return of making her go because they didn't want her.

52. There were other daytime visits on the 21st and 28th July, the latter for a whole day and on this occasion she was reluctant to go until reassured she would not have to stay overnight. On the 4th August she went to stay for two nights after a considerable scene before she would go but on her return Miss Lees thought she had enjoyed herself. On the 13th, she went to stay for three nights but at 7.45 the next morning she turned up again on the doorstep of her aunt Mrs. Shirley, to whom she had run in June. She was half-dressed, barefoot, carrying all her clothes and very distressed. She told Mrs. Shirley she had run away and kept talking about going back to the Coopers. She was taken there and collected again from there by Mrs. Kepple who shook and slapped her "to make her understand it was wrong to run away". No doubt this recurrence of Maria running away worried Mrs. Kepple and was certainly re-

sponsible for her later practice of locking the child in her bedroom. On her return after the visit Miss Lees thought Maria happy enough but rather subdued.

54. By September the pattern was becoming well established. Regular visits were planned including visits direct from school and Maria's resistance was becoming more strenuous, resulting in major scenes on nearly every occasion. Two visits had to be cancelled because she had worked herself into such a state of kicking and screaming that Miss Lees realised it was impossible to insist. On the second of those occasions she struggled so hard with Mr. Cooper who was trying to put her into the car that she was almost beside herself, biting and pulling his hair. On the other hand, it seemed that once arrived at the Kepples Maria tended to calm down and to enjoy the company of her siblings as well as continuing to forge an improved relationship with her mother.

55. By September at Middle Street Junior School Maria's class teacher was Mrs. Locke. She told us that when she first knew Maria she was a clean, well fed, placid, quiet, sweet and happy child. She knew Maria's return to her mother was planned because Mrs. Cooper had told her so at the start of the term. It is worth noting that she told us that Mrs. Cooper came very often to the school, more so than other parents. Mrs. Locke also met Miss Lees who told her that trial weekends were planned for Maria with her mother to see how things went and she was a witness to a good deal of the distress and scenes on several occasions when Maria was collected from the school to go on visits. Mrs. Locke assumed the authorities knew what they were doing but told us that she thought it seemed a very inhuman procedure.

56. On the 27th September after Maria had spent a weekend at the Kepples she returned with bruising in the

form of distinct finger marks on her thigh and she told the
Coopers that "the man who lived with Pauline had done it".
Mrs. Cooper told us she told Miss Lees about this and it is
clear she is right because there is a reference to it in Miss
Lees' notes, but it is there said that it was Mrs. Kepple who
hit her. Mrs. Kepple had also said something to Maria
about picking her up again on the Monday after school.
That day Maria ran away again, this time from school, and
in our minds the only possible inference was fear of another
visit. She asked Mrs. Locke if she could go to the lavatory
and promptly disappeared, leaving her coat and lunch behind. The police were informed and when they went to the
Coopers Maria was found hiding in the bathroom, unknown to
her foster parents. On the 29th September Mrs. Locke had to
take Maria to the car to persuade her to go with her
mother and Miss Lees recognised that Mrs. Kepple's other
child who was present did not help matters by continually
chanting "My mummy is going to get you—you are coming
back for good."

     57. By 1st October East Sussex learnt that Mrs.
Kepple had been advised by her solicitor to apply at once
for revocation of the care order. . . .

     59. It is clear if one looks at the history of that
summer and autumn as a whole that the laudable intention
of East Sussex expressed in April to gain time was frustrated
by the march of events. The increased visiting was pro-
ducing increased resistance from and trauma for Maria, although the social workers comforted themselves with the
belief, undoubtedly genuine and possibly justified, that she
was building a satisfactory relationship with her mother and
enjoyed the younger children. Mrs. Kepple, apparently
now pushed by Mr. Kepple, was not prepared to hold off
making her application to the Court any longer. The social
workers' view of Maria's distress and resistance may be

summed up succinctly as (1) being due to her fear of losing
the Coopers rather than any fear or dislike of the Kepple
household, and (2) that in any event it was within expected
and well recognised limits in such circumstances. Nor was
Miss Lees prepared to admit at the Inquiry that the independent views of a medical man such as a psychiatrist, had
one been consulted about Maria's attitude, could have added
anything to the picture that would have assisted her, and
presumably this was also her senior officer's opinion (Miss
Coulthard). Miss Lees said that because of the tensions in
the situation she had to make an intelligent guess as to
Maria's true feelings. We were also told that the sort of
scenes outlined above are quite common when this sort of
"transfer of loyalties"—as it was described—is being attempted. While we accept that a certain amount of distress
may be unavoidable, we cannot accept that in a case such
as this a child should be subjected to the degree of stress
shown by Maria. Nor do we consider an intelligent guess as
to the cause of that stress to be sufficient in this case.

60.   We find it difficult to understand why Miss Lees
took the view she did about seeking psychiatric or paediatric
advice at this time. We appreciate that social work training
contains an element of child psychology. Surely, however,
such training should enable social workers to turn readily
for specialist help when severe trauma presents, so that
medical skill can supplement their own casework skill.

62.   The position had clearly been reached, as was
anticipated in April, that the tension for Maria was ap-
proaching an unacceptable level whatever the true cause of
it. That was the view of Dr. White Franklin in evidence and
to that extent he and East Sussex were in agreement. That
meant that a decision one way or the other had to be made,
and by October [1971] it was known that Mrs. Kepple's
application would be heard in the near future. If the de-

cision was made not to oppose her it would mean that it was highly probable that the Court would revoke the care order and Maria would go back with only a very short trial period of a month behind her. It was agreed by East Sussex that this was not a moment which they would have chosen to hand Maria back. Moreover, it was accepted that a longer trial period was desirable followed by an assessment of the position. Dr. White Franklin's view was that six months was a minimum. Yet East Sussex decided not to oppose. Their reasoning appeared to be that if Mrs. Kepple did not succeed on this first occasion she would probably do so sooner or later and therefore it was better to accept the position and seek to control it. . . . [T]his belief of theirs was genuinely held and, moreover, in accordance with the current climate of opinion we are quite prepared to accept. There is no doubt that it was generally believed that natural parents had the "right" to have their child back from care once they had established that they were fit to receive it and that this thinking influenced magistrates courts. Nevertheless, it seems to us that it was implicit in the April decision, and reinforced by the evidence that it was not a moment chosen to return Maria, that East Sussex ought to have made every effort to gain time for a longer trial period of assessment to take place. . . .

64. . . . On Friday the 22nd [of October] Mr. Cooper took Maria to Middle Street School for the last time. She was nicely dressed and brought a box of chocolates for her school friends. Later Mr. Cooper collected her and took her to the Hove Social Services Office whence Miss Coulthard (Miss Lees' senior, who had taken over from Mr. Bennett since the April conference) took her to the Kepples. She had screamed and clung to Mr. Cooper at the office and was apprehensive about going with her mother who was present. She was given an assurance by Mrs. Kepple in Miss

Coulthard's presence that she would be returning to the Coopers at the weekend. We think this was inexcusable. She then went quietly and on that false note her new life began. She was never to see the Coopers again.

65.   Shortly after moving to her mother's, on the Monday, Maria again ran away to her aunt Mrs. Shirley. It is impossible to resist the inference that there was a connection between this choice of day and her discovery of her mother's deceit. She arrived on Mrs. Shirley's doorstep at 7.45 A.M. wearing only a dirty T-shirt and trousers. She was barefoot, crying and in a very distressed state. She repeatedly said "don't let me go" and wanted to go back to her mummy and daddy. Miss Lees was telephoned and came round. Maria continued to cry and said she wanted to go back to "mummy and daddy Cooper" and begged not to be sent back to Pauline. When Mrs. Kepple appeared to claim her Maria cringed, according to Mrs. Shirley. Miss Lees thought she calmed down quite well and allowed herself to be dressed and taken home where she was quite "bright and chatty".

66.   It is obvious to us, as was Dr. White Franklin's opinion, that the child had very strong feelings and was demonstrating them in a significant way. The doctor also gave it as his opinion that for practical purposes at this time Maria was a part of the Cooper family. Moreover, in his view to remove a child after such a period of time would be a very dangerous thing to do unless she had an equal relationship with the people to whom she was going. He also told us that the so-called "blood tie" was a totally inadequate substitute if this had not been present when the child was developing. It is not necessary for us to pronounce upon the application of these latter principles to the present case, nor appropriate for us to express any view of their general validity. What we do consider wholly wrong is that no effort,

even at that late stage, was made to obtain a medical opinion as to the depth and significance of Maria's continuing protests.

67.   On the 17th November the Hove Juvenile Court heard Mrs. Kepple's application. Mrs. Kepple was legally represented and gave the only evidence that was called. The Court had a full report from Miss Lees on behalf of the local authority and we accept that of its kind it was probably of the standard expected in general terms. It was also, we accept, intended by Miss Lees to be fair and in no way to mislead the Court. It made clear that the East Sussex decision not to oppose was not an easy or clear-cut one, and it concluded by recommending that a supervision order might replace the care order with Mrs. Kepple resuming her parental responsibilities. Unfortunately, in our view, but entirely naturally in view of Miss Lees' interpretation of Maria's protests and trauma, it put a gloss on that aspect of the matter which distorted the true picture. It referred to Maria's last running away to Mrs. Shirley but made no mention of the previous three occasions and referred to her "confusion over where her loyalties lie". To our mind, there was never at any time upon the evidence before us, any doubt at all where Maria's loyalties lay, and that was with the Coopers. On that ground the report can be criticised, but it is important to realise that this only arises because of the social workers' assumptions about the trauma, which we have already indicated they were not qualified to make on their own in the particular circumstances of this case. . . . Since it has been admitted in evidence that this was not a moment when, unless forced by events, East Sussex would have chosen to return Maria, it seems to us that the omission of this factor from Miss Lees' report was also a mistake. The Court was entitled to know this.

68.   One other matter which arose at the hearing

should be noted. At some point in her evidence Mrs. Kepple was clearly asked the question—whether by her solicitor or the Court cannot be determined—what was Mr. Kepple's attitude to Maria, because her answer is recorded by the clerk as "he treats Maria as one of his own children". This was in direct contradiction of Miss Lees' observation of him as recently as July when she considered that he impressed as a man who would not be very accepting of another man's children. No doubt had the case been a contested one that point would have been picked up and the matter probed in cross-examination. Miss Lees was in a very difficult position before the Court because of the multiplicity of roles she was obliged to play. . . .

That of advocate was not officially amongst them, but one assumes that any conscientious social worker would not allow a piece of evidence to go unchallenged by an applicant in Mrs. Kepple's position if she disagreed with it. This was clearly an important question and answer especially as little was said about Mr. Kepple in Court and he was not present. Miss Lees, however, told us that she did not think the evidence meant any more than whether Mr. Kepple was accepting the same responsibility for Maria as for his own children, which was of course a much narrower question. If she misinterpreted the matter in that way she cannot be blamed for not intervening. This would be a difficult task in any event, which prompts us to indicate our view that in a difficult case such as this one, even if the application is not contested, legal representation on both sides is helpful. It is not for us to consider the much wider and more radical proposition of independent representation for the child.

69. The Coopers were not told the date of the hearing, and were not present; nor were they told the result. They had no right in law to be notified as they were not

"parties" to the proceedings, and unless needed as witnesses by a party [had] no right to give evidence. . . .

18 November 1971 to 31 March 1972*

77. [Miss Lees continued to have supervisory authority over Maria, although the documentary evidence only supported proof of two visits prior to February 15.] The six monthly report referred to is fairly noncommittal in its terms but records that "Maria's return to her mother seems to have been more successful than might have been anticipated". It also contains the sentence "Maria has put on weight since returning to her mother" which was based upon no more than Miss Lees' observation of the child and in our view should not have been phrased in factual terms. Maria's last medical examination under the care order had been on the 4 August 1971 and as a result there was no base line data coinciding precisely with her return to her mother by which her subsequent progress or possible regression could be measured. More of Miss Lees' thoughts on the success of the child's return are to be found in a "summary to date" under the entry for 15 February in her case notes: "Maria continues to make progress with the Kepples . . . she has grown taller and has been very quiet when I have visited . . . I feel she is not altogether a happy child, but has settled better than might be expected . . . she shows considerable affection towards her mother . . . Mr. Kepple still favours his own although claims this is not so. Maria showed little attachment to him."

The Events of April 1972

81. At some time in either March or April 1972 Mrs. Rickwood, who lived at 99 Maresfield Road and had a

---

* From [paragraph 70] to paragraph 148, Miss Stevenson agrees with the narrative as presented by the Committee.

little daughter who used to play with Maria, took both children to Eastbourne for the day and it appears that Maria may well have gone without Mrs. Kepple's knowledge or at least consent. The following day when Mrs. Rickwood went up to see Mrs. Kepple the latter gave Maria a severe slap by way of a back-hander across the face which rather shocked Mrs. Rickwood and thereafter the latter had seen bruises on Maria's face from time to time, notably, she told us, in April, May and towards the end of July. . . .

84. On Wednesday the 12 April Mrs. Rutson was . . . in her back garden pegging out some washing. She had felt concern for Maria . . . because nothing had been seen of the child since [April 3] and the curtains of the bedroom which Maria occupied had been drawn ever since. The front and back doors of 119 had often been left open and the other Kepple children had gone in and out. It was school holiday time and a period when children might be expected to be playing about the place out of doors, and Mrs. Rutson feared Maria might be locked in her bedroom. While in her garden on that Wednesday Mrs. Rutson looked up at the bedroom of number 119 with the drawn curtain and saw Maria looking out of the side of the curtain. Her face was, she told us, "terribly blackened and she had a terribly bloodshot eye—one eye was just a pool of blood." . . .

85. [Mrs. Rutson telephoned the NSPCC and related her observations and fears about Maria.] The NSPCC inspector at that time was Mrs. Kirby who was carrying a double load of responsibility because although the area's establishment was supposed to be two inspectors a vacancy created in 1970 had not yet been filled and she was having to cope with the area on her own. The message did not reach her until the morning of Friday the 14 April. It must be a matter for comment that when the Society's precept in its

directives to its inspectors concerning "Investigation of Complaints" reads: "all complaints . . . must be inquired into immediately," the administrative arrangements then in force prevented any on-the-spot investigation by Mrs. Kirby until almost 24 hours after Mrs. Rutson's complaint was received. It is pertinent to observe here that none of the agencies concerned with what one might conveniently call "the April incident" in our view moved with a sufficient sense of urgency, not only because of the possible threat to Maria's continued safety but, equally important, because if drastic action and even criminal proceedings might become necessary then it was vital that medical opinion be sought without delay before the evidence of the bruising and injured eye literally faded or disappeared. Every day was of importance and the longer it was before the child was medically examined the less help could be expected from a doctor.

86.   Mrs. Kirby began her investigation by discovering that Maria was under the supervision of Miss Lees to whom she imparted on the phone the substance of the complaint she had received and they decided upon a joint visit to the Kepples that afternoon. When they arrived at 119 Maresfield Road they found Mrs. Kepple and the other children present but not Maria, who was said by Mrs. Kepple to be at the dentist with Mr. Kepple. Mrs. Kirby made plain to her the nature of the complaint that had been received and Mrs. Kepple told her visitors that they had better talk to Mr. Kepple because Maria had not been hit and was perfectly all right. . . .

87.   Miss Lees and Mrs. Kirby, having been told the address of the dentist, proceeded there only to find that the dentist had never heard of the child. Upon returning to number 119 they were confronted by a furious Mr. Kepple who hurled abuse at Miss Lees. Of Maria there was still no sign,

nor now of Mrs. Kepple, who according to Mr. Kepple had
taken Maria shopping. This explanation was rapidly followed by another. *i.e.*, that Mrs. Kepple had taken Maria to
Miss Lees' office. This also was a lie but Miss Lees because
of pressure of work left the house at about 4.30 P.M. to return to her office. There was no sign of Maria and Mrs.
Kepple. Mrs. Kirby, with Miss Lees' knowledge, decided to
sit it out. At some point in the interview Mr. Kepple, who
was loquacious throughout, volunteered the information that
Maria had "a little bruise on her face". [B]y no stretch
of the imagination could the visible injuries on the child at
that time be so described.

88.   He also told Mrs. Kirby that Maria had fallen
off her scooter down the steps. At 5.45 P.M. Mrs. Kirby had
to leave but informed Mr. Kepple that she would be returning later which she did at 8 P.M., by which time Mrs. Kepple
and Maria were also present. Mrs. Kirby's observations of
the injuries confirmed those of Mrs. Rutson of two days before, *i.e.* bruises on both sides of the face and the right eye
very bloodshot. Maria was told to tell Mrs. Kirby how she
had hurt herself and she told her that she had fallen on her
scooter down the front steps, and Mrs. Kepple added that
this had happened on the previous Monday (the 10th). Although aware of the possibility that the child was repeating
what she had been told to say, Mrs. Kirby thought this was
a feasible explanation—the buckled scooter was produced
for her inspection and she thought Maria was telling the
truth. She therefore thought there was no further immediate
action required of her.

93.   [Two days later] Mrs. Rutson heard the Kep-
ples arguing in their garden about which of them had struck
Maria, each blaming the other. This clearly impressed Mrs.
Rutson—as indeed it did us, since the logic of such an argu-

ment was that since neither was alleging an accident one or other was guilty—and that evening she visited Mrs. Kirby's home and left a message for her because of her continuing anxiety as to what was happening to Maria. Later that evening she received a message asking her to see Mrs. Kirby the next afternoon—Monday the 17th.

94. On the Monday at 9.30 A.M. a phone call reached the Brighton Social Services Department from a Mr. Parsons of 125 Maresfield Road who gave them an account of the previous day's incident and stated that the little girl concerned (he did not know her previously or her name) had been beaten or otherwise ill-treated and locked in her bedroom. He left his name and address but no one communicated with him again. . . .

95. That same afternoon (Monday the 17th) Miss Lees, Mrs. Rutson and Mrs. Kirby met at the latter's house and there was a discussion about Maria lasting at least two hours, during which Miss Lees explained the background of the whole matter to Mrs. Rutson who was still gravely concerned over Maria, and clearly giving expression to that concern coupled with misgivings over how the matter was being handled. According to Mrs. Rutson, at some point in the interview she asked the other two what explanation the Kepples had given and she was told that they had said Maria had fallen downstairs with a scooter; whereupon Mrs. Rutson had asked if Miss Lees was satisfied with that explanation and she told us she had got the reply: "Well, knowing the family, I would say that Maria has had a beating." Miss Lees told us that she was sure she would not have said "beating" but might have used the expression "backhander". . . .

96. . . . What matters, it seems to us, is that Miss Lees, who had not yet seen Maria, did not convey to Mrs.

Rutson any impression that she was seriously concerned. We think that she may not have appreciated the possible inference to be drawn from the fact of the Kepples arguing over which of them had struck Maria. In addition, she clearly had reservations about accepting Mrs. Rutson's account of events in its entirety because she considered that while Mrs. Rutson was very genuinely concerned about Maria her attitude was coloured, *inter alia,* by her view of different standards of bringing up children. Moreover, it appears from Mr. McBurney's notes that later that month Miss Lees told him that she felt that the Rutsons and other neighbours did not have Maria's well-being in mind when complaints were made. If Miss Lees' reservations about Mrs. Rutson in turn "coloured" her reaction to events this was very unfortunate, for as we know Mrs. Rutson's account of events was substantially accurate.

97.   Mrs. Kirby, after the interview at least, was no longer under any misapprehension of the seriousness of the position and the inference to be drawn from the Sunday row between the Kepples, because her case notes record: "It is quite apparent one of them is the culprit, this could easily be Mrs. Kepple, she is said to go into the most outrageous frenzies and can be heard screaming and swearing." By the end of the interview Miss Lees had clearly given both Mrs. Kirby and Mrs. Rutson to understand that she would ensure that the child was taken to a doctor who would be warned first as to the reasons for the examination. . . . Mrs. Kirby told us that if she had thought the child was not going to see a doctor she would not have left the matter there and we accept that. Mrs. Rutson, on leaving, was asked to get in touch with Miss Lees or Mrs. Kirby if necessary in future.

98.   The following day, Tuesday the 18 April, Miss Lees visited the Kepples and saw Maria. She was unsure in

her evidence as to whether she discussed the injury with Maria, *i.e.* heard any explanation from her own lips, but the inference is that if she had got any such explanation she would have noted it. By this time the bruising was fading fast but the eye was still rather bloodshot. . . .

99. Miss Lees only "advised" Mrs. Kepple to take Maria to the doctor and did not "ensure" that the child was medically examined. . . .

103. On or about the 24 April a deputation of the Kepples' neighbours complained to Mr. Smith of Brighton Housing Department under whose aegis came the administration of the Whitehawk estate. The complaints were of ill-treatment of Maria. . . . He and Miss Lees in fact met later on the 24th and clearly they had a long discussion about the case generally. Their discussion included a decision that Brighton might be able to assist the family materially; Mrs. Kirby's involvement which had been arranged with Miss Lees was notified to Mr. McBurney and Miss Lees told him also that she was very mindful of Brighton's legal responsibility but she wished to persevere with the placement of Maria and continue to supervise.

May to November 1972

106. In May Miss Dean [Maria's teacher] noticed, as indeed had several neighbours of the Kepples, a bruise close to her eye, and on examining it she saw it had three lines which appeared to be like finger marks and she naturally questioned her about it. With marked reluctance and only after repeated questions Maria said: "my little brother hit me with the Hoover". [Mrs. Kepple's written evidence to us was that there was a toy of this nature in the house.] This seemed so odd an explanation to Miss Dean that she took Maria to the headmistress Miss Coo and the welfare

assistant Mrs. Tharme and made her repeat her story, which she did. The consensus of view of the three ladies was that this was not really an acceptable explanation and Maria was being loyal to someone. If this information had reached either the Social Services Department—the school knew of Miss Lees' interest in the child from previous contacts—or Mrs. Kirby, as it should have done, coming so soon after the injuries involved in the April incident it must have prompted increased concern and supervision at the least. Unfortunately, this did not happen. It may be convenient here to carry forward to the end of the summer term the impression Miss Dean and Miss Coo had of Maria's general state of well-being, which was that whereas she had been of average height on arrival, by July she did not seem to have grown like the others and had become one of the smallest in the class. She had also become listless, tired and unkempt and was no longer well dressed or groomed, and it was noticed how voraciously she ate her school meals. Unfortunately, the arrangements under which Maria would have had a school medical examination in the spring term of 1972 had changed that year to an autumn term examination. . . .

107. On the 1 June Miss Lees visited the Kepples and took Mrs. Kepple and the children out shopping to get some new clothes for Maria. All seemed well and Miss Lees noted that "it was a happy expedition and the family presented as a fairly close unit". This was to be the last time Miss Lees saw Maria for exactly six months, until the 1 December. Although she visited once more on the 16 June she did not see Maria on that occasion and for one reason or another there were no more effective visits until December. This seems to us to be a complete failure to supervise over this period for which Miss Lees' seniors must share her responsibility and which was probably largely due to three factors: (a) the initial failure to diagnose the gravity of the

situation during April; (*b*) the fact that information of
events after April was not getting through to Miss Lees;
(*c*) the belief of Miss Lees that Mrs. Kirby was regularly
visiting. There was some evidence that later during this
period Mrs. Kepple was aware that all was not well with
Maria and was trying to communicate this to outside sources,
and had Miss Lees visited this anxiety might well have
reached her.

110. During August Mrs. Rutson telephoned the
NSPCC to inform them she had seen bruises on Maria, in
response to Mrs. Kirby's invitation in April to let her know
if necessary anything about Maria. That message never
reached Mrs. Kirby, nor did another call by Mrs. Rutson in
either September or October. . . .

111. It is time to turn to the Kepples' neighbours
and record briefly their observations of how Maria was being treated and how she appeared to them over the whole
period from April until the autumn. There was abundant
evidence of a steady deterioration in Maria's appearance,
both physical and otherwise, her bearing and her treatment.
The evidence of Mrs. Ward who lived just across the road
was typical. She recalled how "pert and nice" Maria had
been when she came to live at number 119; she had been well
dressed and happy and had played and mixed well with
other children up to about the spring of 1972; then she had
become unkempt and started to stand alone, watching the
others play. She began to get extremely thin in the face and
legs and appeared terribly frightened; she ran and jumped
to attention when her mother screamed at her and became
increasingly withdrawn. Finally, Mrs. Ward stressed Maria's
"desperate depression; to me it seemed to be laid right across
her forehead and she was never free of it". There was evidence, which we accept, of several incidents when Mrs.
Kepple lost her temper with Maria and struck her with con-

siderable severity. There was abundant evidence of discrimination against Maria in the good things in a child's life such as ice cream, sweets and oranges, her siblings being given them while she was omitted unless a friendly neighbour came forward to redress the balance. There was a substantial body of evidence which satisfied us that not only was Maria running errands to the shops, which of itself would not excite any comment in that community, but that it caused her lateness at school which started again in the autumn term, and also that she was having to struggle home with 28 lb. bags of coal, which must then have been equal to about two-thirds of her own weight. So incensed did Mrs. Jenkins, the shopkeeper who sold the coal, become with the sight of Maria having to struggle up the very steep hill from the shop, that she sent a message to Mrs. Kepple that unless some sort of conveyance was provided in future she would cease to serve Maria. Thereafter an outsize pram was provided over which the child could hardly see and which must have improved the task but little.

113.   On the 18 August Mrs. Kirby paid a home visit to the Kepples of which she recorded a very full note. Her conclusion was that Maria appeared to be fit and well but certain other observations of hers were significant in retrospect. . . . Mrs. Kirby . . . noted that Maria was not playing with the other children who ran in and out but just stood by the steps outside. Mrs. Kepple told her that although Maria had a good appetite they were worried because she was so thin, and also that the Coopers had appeared in the road the previous week and taken her for a ride, asking her a lot of questions. There was no truth in this latter piece of information at all. Maria had indeed told her mother this story about the Coopers but it is clear she was merely living for the moment in a dream world of fantasy, recreating the presence of those she loved and had been parted from. . . .

115. In September Maria started at Whitehawk Junior School where her class teacher was Mrs. Turner, who although a probationary teacher in her first term was an SRN and a mother of five children. . . .

120. Half-term at Maria's school was at the end of October and the second half was due to begin on the 6 November. During the first two weeks of that period Maria missed two days altogether, was late on three other days and attended school for the last time on Friday the 17th. During those two weeks her teacher Mrs. Turner became increasingly concerned about Maria and her general state of health and, of course, being herself a mother of five children and also a trained nurse, was well equipped to observe her condition. She considered Maria to be very withdrawn, and becoming more so, as though living in a world of her own and very thin. On one occasion when Maria was crying she had taken her on her knee to comfort her only to be shocked at realising by this first physical contact just how thin she was. She likened the sensation in a telling phrase to holding a bird in one's hand and being frightened to hold it too tight in case one squeezed the life out of it. In addition, Maria's ravenous appetite at school meals had been noticed by the staff and Mrs. Turner wondered, as that appeared to be the child's only daily meal, whether on those occasions when she was absent from school she was being fed at all. She had not, however, seen bruises on her and never did.

122. On the 13 November Maria was late for school again and gave as the reason that she had to go to shop for coal, bread and potatoes, and Mrs. Dickinson visited that day but received no reply. On the 14th she called again and saw Mrs. Kepple whom she asked if she sent Maria shopping for coal and potatoes. Mrs. Kepple denied this and said that Maria had a vivid imagination and that she wished people would take no notice of her romancing. As we have already

stated, we entirely accept the evidence of Mrs. Jenkins and several other witnesses that Maria was regularly sent on such errands. Mrs. Turner had naturally been greatly shocked at the thought of a child of Maria's age and size hauling 28 lb. bags of coal up a steep hill and her fears were increased a day or two later when Maria came up to her and said, "Mummy says I have to tell you I did not go to the shop for coal, but honestly I did, Mrs. Turner."

123. When Maria's final absence from school began on Monday the 20 November Mrs. Dickinson continued to visit. We should record here that she and other callers at 119 Maresfield Road—including Miss Lees—experienced difficulty on many occasions in making contact with anyone at the house although suspecting that one or other of the Kepples was inside but preferred not to answer the door. . . . On the 29th Mrs. Dickinson was able to see Mr. Kepple, who explained Maria's continuous absence since the 20th as being due to a bad stomach upset accompanied by severe diarrhoea and vomiting, adding that she could not leave the lavatory for a minute she was running so badly. Mrs. Dickinson said she must have a medical certificate and when she asked to see Maria she was told that despite her supposed illness she was out with Mrs. Kepple. We are quite satisfied that this story of violent illness as the reason for absence from school was untrue. . . .

124. By the end of November a large number of individual threads in the story were beginning to come together. Of Mrs. Turner's anxieties we have spoken; these and rumours among the children that Maria was locked in had reached Mrs. Dickinson, who although initially concerned on the question of non-attendance at school had clearly formed a very unfavourable view of the Kepples and suspected there might be sinister reasons behind Maria's ab-

sences and lateness. At the end of November Mrs. Rutson
rang the school to ask why Maria was not attending. Miss
Lees, who had last seen Maria on the 1 June had, of course,
been assuming that all was well because of the informal
arrangement she had entered into with Mrs. Kirby and had
heard nothing to the contrary. It is right to point out that
no complaints or adverse reports were reaching her at any
rate until November. On the 9 November, however, she had
visited Mrs. Tester to see the two children fostered with her
after an unheralded and unsuccessful visit to the Kepples
and Mrs. Tester had told her that Maria had lost so much
weight that she had hardly recognised her. In view of this
report, which must have concerned Miss Lees, it is surprising
that it was not until the 17th that she wrote to Mrs. Kepple
asking if it would be convenient to pay a visit on the 20th.
It was not convenient for Mrs. Kepple and of course if
Maria was bruised at that time one can see why. . . .

The Last Period from 1 December 1972

125.   On the 1 December Miss Lees visited and saw
Maria and considered her a little taller but very thin, rather
pale and listless. She was impressed that she had lost "a
tremendous amount of weight". Mrs. Kepple told her the
child had had persistent diarrhoea and Maria confirmed this,
but we have already commented upon our view of the seriousness of this alleged illness. She also had a recurrence
of her head infection and Miss Lees considered the loss of
weight could be accounted for by the diarrhoea and she advised Mrs. Kepple to seek medical help for that and the
infection. . . .

126.   If she got in touch at this stage with the school
she would, one hopes, have been in contact with Mrs. Dickinson, who had been greatly and increasingly concerned

over Maria, and either the headmaster or deputy and through them with Mrs. Turner whose anxieties we have referred to. It so happened that on the same day that Miss Lees was visiting the Kepples, *i.e.* the 1 December, Mrs. Dickinson had taken her worries to Brighton Social Services Department where she had been seen by the duty officer Mrs. Hodgson. The latter's note clearly expresses Mrs. Dickinson's concern and records that Maria was not at school and the implication was that she might have been beaten; moreover, her appearance suggested malnutrition. Mrs. Hodgson had a phone conversation at about that time with Mrs. Kirby, for her note records that the latter was supposed to be visiting that day and was "aware that Maria has been beaten before", but Mrs. Hodgson added the extraordinary statement: "I stressed that it was definitely Mrs. Kirby's territory if there was a suspicion of ill-treatment". If this was the considered view of any responsible officer of the Brighton Social Services Department it discloses an unfortunate confusion of thought as to roles and the existence of any line of demarcation between that department and the NSPCC.

130.   The 5th and 6th of December were days of considerable activity by those concerned with Maria's welfare but unhappily there was a lack of cohesive effort in many respects and because of the fatal failure to pool the total knowledge of Maria's background, recent history and physical and mental condition the last real opportunity of removing her was missed. Inevitably, because of the reports reaching the various agencies in 1972 about Maria being bruised it seems certain that the social workers concerned were thinking in terms of child battering, and of course it is true that Maria died from that cause only a month later. When the various persons who examined Maria in Decem-

ber did so they were looking for bruising and other evidence
of physical ill-treatment. When they failed to find it they,
and each and every person who was relying upon those
examinations, were greatly relieved.

131. Had the knowledge and experience of what had
been going on since at least early April . . . been properly
circulated it is inconceivable in our view that Maria would
have been left with the Kepples until her death in January
1973. Those of the neighbours who made complaints to the
authorities might certainly be expected to feel they had fully
played their part. Others relied upon the conscience and
initiative of the few and especially upon Mrs. Rutson. Unfortunately these complaints did not produce the desired result. On the morning of the 5 December Mrs. Dickinson,
who had never been able to see Maria since July despite her
efforts, again visited number 119 having ascertained that
Maria had not attended school. She was confronted by Mr.
Kepple who brandished a strap in the air during the interview with the clear intention of intimidating her. He was
extremely angry and hostile and swore at her. He said it was
no weather to send Maria out and when Mrs. Dickinson
insisted in her official capacity that she must have a medical
certificate or she would bring him before the Education
Committee, he said Maria was in bed. When Mrs. Dickinson said she would not leave until she had seen her Mr.
Kepple replied that she was out with Mrs. Kepple at the
doctor's. When Mrs. Dickinson said she would phone the
doctor he said she had gone shopping, and when Mrs. Dickinson said she would go and look for her because she had to
keep her appointment at the school clinic he then said she
had gone to Portslade for the day. At the conclusion of the
interview he said he would make an appointment with the
doctor and take the child himself, and added "you will get

your medical certificate" before slamming the door. Once again Mr. Kepple had shown something of himself and his attitude towards authority.

132. Mrs. Dickinson went straight to her senior officer Mrs. Tattam and made a report to her which she followed up with a written report three days later. Mrs. Tattam at once phoned East Sussex and spoke to someone unknown, Miss Lees being then unavailable, but she received the message and decided upon a visit that very afternoon. Because she considered it might prove necessary to apply at once for a place of safety order and the matter was within Brighton's jurisdiction she co-ordinated her visit with the Brighton duty officer Mr. Rutherford and went with him to 119 Maresfield Road in the early afternoon. No answer was obtained and Miss Lees tried again later in the afternoon, this time with Mr. McBurney who, however, remained in the car outside ready to assist if necessary. What Miss Lees found completely reassured her. She was able to see Maria stripped on the pretext of looking to see if the skin infection had spread and saw no signs of bruising. Mrs. Kepple showed her some medicine and ointment she had obtained from the doctor for Maria and Miss Lees considered the child more lively than on her previous visit four days before. In fact, Maria had not seen the doctor at that time and whatever Mrs. Kepple showed Miss Lees it had not been recently prescribed for her, if indeed it ever had been.

140. On 9 December Mr. Kepple phoned the NSPCC to say that Maria could not attend the children's party given by the Society on that day as her skin complaint had not cleared up. By the 11th Maria had still not returned to school and Mrs. Dickinson again visited number 119. Either Mr. or Mrs. Kepple had left a message at the school that Maria had a bad stomach, but Mrs. Dickinson was

unable to get any reply although she called three times on that day and again on 13 December. The day before Mrs. Rutson had decided to make yet another attempt to alert the authorities to Maria's unsatisfactory condition. She had seen her in the back garden looking "more or less like a skeleton", unkempt and dirty, and she telephoned Miss Lees. Unfortunately Miss Lees was not available and Mrs. Rutson left her name and her sister's telephone number—she having no telephone at home—so that Miss Lees could ring back. Although the telephone was not left unattended that day or the next no call came. Miss Lees told us that she got the message and did try to telephone but received no answer, and assumed that if the matter was important Mrs. Rutson would ring again. Miss Lees tried again next day but was unsuccessful. There the matter rested and clearly the explanations of what went wrong might be found in several different causes—it is impossible to tell which is the correct one. . . .

141. The 13 December saw Maria still away from school and Mrs. Dickinson's last, and still unsuccessful, visit. Nobody could fault her for perseverance but she was operating in isolation from the other social services and in our view here again there was a lack of co-ordinated effort. At this vital time neither she nor Mrs. Tattam nor Miss Bodger were in contact with Miss Lees. On that day the latter paid another visit to the Kepples which further reassured her. The whole family were present and Maria seemed much improved but still very thin and Miss Lees was pleased to hear her spontaneously and for the first time call Mr. Kepple "dad". She discussed possible child guidance for Maria with Mrs. Kepple and also considered a possible later referral to the children's hospital if her physical condition did not improve. In conclusion Miss Lees felt very much happier about

the family. The only discordant and probably significant note in retrospect was the fact that Mrs. Kepple was not very anxious for Miss Lees to speak to Maria on her own. It is greatly to be regretted that none of the several people intimately concerned with Maria's welfare and happiness, except for Mrs. Turner to a limited degree, were able to reach through to her real feelings. It is perhaps fair to Miss Lees to draw particular attention to the fact that she was at this time considering referral of Maria not only to the Child Guidance Clinic but to the children's hospital. It is the tragedy of this case that fate intervened before she had decided the moment was right.

143.   On Monday 18 December at 2.45 P.M. another anonymous caller telephoned the NSPCC to complain that Maria had been seen the previous week with her face all marked with bruises again. This report did not reach Mrs. Kirby until the following day. This was another unnecessary delay. She did not investigate the matter according to standing orders but 'phoned Miss Lees and told her, and entered this in her notes. Miss Lees, strangely, had neither record nor recollection of this. . . .

145.   At this point it is helpful to refer to a statement put in as evidence by Mrs. Kepple, who did not give oral evidence before us. Although, of course, not subject to cross-examination, it contained much that bore to us at least the ring of truth. In it she recalled Maria's steady deterioration; how she got thinner and as she did so became more dreamy and quiet and went about in a daze; how she would not answer anyone but would sit and stare into space; how her habits of personal cleanliness greatly changed for the worse; how Mrs. Kepple thought she was pining for the Coopers and how she even became destructive of her own clothes. The whole picture drawn by Mrs. Kepple of Maria during the last few months of her life is a startling cor-

roboration of, and wholly consistent with, the outward signs as observed by the neighbours.

146. Maria was not seen alive outside the circle of her own family after Sandra Tester's visit on 27 December and we have only Mrs. Kepple's unchallenged account of those last days, but we feel some aspects of it should be recorded. In brief she told us that on 2 January 1973 she returned to find Maria with a black eye and Mr. Kepple told her she had fallen downstairs. Two days later she alleged that Mr. Kepple started hitting Maria on her legs because she had not used paper in the lavatory and she had tried to stop him and he had been very angry with her also. She had, she told us, made up her mind to tell Miss Lees, having already told Mr. Kepple that she would tell her that he and Maria didn't get on. However, on 6 January, which was a Saturday, Mr. Kepple came in at 11.30 P.M. and the events which formed the basis of the indictment against Mr. Kepple then occurred.

147. The following morning the Kepples took Maria in the pram to the hospital where she was found to be dead. The post mortem carried out by Professor Cameron on 11 January showed that she was severely bruised all over the body and head and had sustained severe internal injuries to the stomach. There was a healing fracture of one rib. The bruising, which was described by Professor Cameron as the worst he had ever seen, was of variable age up to 10 to 14 days at most, which was the longest period that bruising might be expected to last, but the majority dated from within 48 hours. The majority of the injuries he described as the result of extreme violence. The stomach was empty and the body weighed 36 lbs., whereas the medical evidence in the case generally showed that she should for her age and height have weighed anything between 46 and 50 lbs. or thereabouts. She had in fact grown one inch and lost over 5

lbs. since her last medical examination on 4 August 1971, 17 months before her death.

148. To conclude the narrative of events, when the "scenes of crime" police officer visited Maria's bedroom at number 119 on the 7 January he found that the door handle was removable so that when the door was closed from the outside anyone inside the room was shut in. Mrs. Kepple in the course of her lengthy interviews with the police subsequently admitted that Maria was from time to time so confined because she was afraid she would run away as she had done before in 1971. Although she denied this admission in her written statement to us we are satisfied that Maria was so confined on occasions.

[The stepfather, William Kepple, was found guilty of Maria's murder in April 1973. Three months later an appeals court substituted a verdict of manslaughter for that of murder and sentenced him to eight years' imprisonment. Mr. Kepple had had a minor criminal record at the time of Maria's transfer—unknown to the caseworkers at the time —that included four cases of violence on two separate occasions.]

COMMENT—HAD OUR GROUNDS BEEN APPLICABLE

According to experience with children at the toddler stage, Maria's first removal from the Coopers, after a stay with them from the age of 4 months to the age of 15 months, must have been deeply upsetting for her. Nevertheless, it was within her mother's rights to remove her, even according to the strict provisions of the grounds that we propose. The fostering arrangement, this time a voluntary one, had lasted no longer than 11 months, thus being by definition "temporary." That, after an almost immediate breakdown of maternal care, and following an unsuitable private placement, she was returned to the familiar aunt and uncle, this time under an official "place of safety" order (October 1966), can be counted to her benefit. What ran counter to her interests was the official long-term aim for eventual return to her mother, a plan which, in fact, did not exclude her staying with the Coopers for the next 5 years (1966–71).

Under our grounds for intervention Maria's official story would have been cut short as early as 1968 when the Coopers first raised the question of adoption. They would have been entitled to this since they had taken care of Maria uninterruptedly for longer than 12 months, i.e., exceeding the statutory period suggested by us for the fostering of a child under 3 years at the time of placement.

However, even if they had made no move in the direction of adoption, or if their application had been denied for one reason or another, their status as long-time caretakers could not have failed to be recognized in 1971 after 5 years of caring for Maria and would have assured them party status and designation as Foster Parents with Tenure in the Hove Juvenile Court hearing of that year. Maria too could have been represented by separate counsel.

Again, if neither adoption nor recognition of foster care with tenure had been in question, and return to the biological mother had been contemplated, our provisions would have precluded subjecting Maria to the agonizing ordeal of experimental (or preparatory) visiting. More vividly than any of our arguments, the Report's description of Maria's reactions demonstrates the shattering effect of this procedure on a child's feeling of security and the stability of her personality in general. While earlier routine visits to the biological mother had remained uneventful, from 1970 onward, when Mrs. Kepple first mentioned her intentions in Maria's presence, the child became uneasy, upset, and distressed. When, with the aim of final return in view, visiting was intensified, she answered with kicking and screaming, clinging, hiding, repeated running away, deterioration in behavior and health. All these should have been taken as unmistakable signs of where her loyalties lay, who her psychological parents were, and that return to her natural mother represented a threat to her well-being. That her negative reaction was ignored and her traumatized state treated as being within the norm for such occasions were decisive steps toward the ultimate tragedy. Had the social services department objected to Maria's return to the Kepples, rather than decided "not to oppose" it, and had these facts been brought before the court, the judge would have been provided with an opportunity and a basis for letting Maria remain with the Coopers.

Under our longtime caretaker ground any information about the biological mother and the stepfather would have been of no importance for the child at this late date (with Maria either adopted by the Coopers or in their foster care with tenure). Under the premises of the Report, however, it was highly relevant. Mrs. Kepple had four children of a first marriage in the care of the local authority under a "place of safety" order, and complaints had been received that the three children of her second marriage, who were living with her, were "unsupervised, unkempt, dirty," and occasionally bruised. Mr. Kepple not only had a drinking problem at the time of Maria's transfer; he also had a minor criminal record, four cases of violence in two separate occasions. Though the evidence was insufficient to justify removing the three Kepple children, it would have been sufficient to preclude the Kepples from qualifying as foster parents or adoptive parents. Had Mrs. Kepple been a stranger without the prerogative accorded to a biological parent, Maria would never have been put into her care.

Finally, during the last 6 months of Maria's life, numerous complaints made by neighbors and the school about her maltreatment reached the social services and National Society for the Prevention of Cruelty to Children. Our grounds, too, would have justified an investigation which could have led to an immediate emergency placement for Maria and to a hearing to determine whether to terminate Mrs. Kepple's parental rights to Maria. Thus, even at this late stage Maria's life might have been saved.

There is no doubt that carefully compiled documents such as the Report on the Care and Supervision of Maria Colwell have much to offer to students of the child placement process.[5] Such reports make it possible to identify step by step the provisions designed to serve as inbuilt safeguards; and to test and give evidence to either their efficacy or inefficacy.

Once the warnings against return to such parents have been disregarded, the fate of children such as Melisha, Karen, Jill, Angelo, and Maria is sealed. No amount of supervision from outside can counteract what happens within the privacy of a family.

Appendix II

Suggestions for Some Provisions of a Child Placement Code

Here we suggest language for statutory provisions to codify some of our proposals. The book itself serves as a commentary to these provisions. They are to be read in the context of and as additions or amendments to the provisions in the Child Placement Code of Hampstead-Haven in Chapter 7 of *Beyond the Best Interests of the Child.**

ARTICLE 10.   DEFINITIONS

PARA. 10.1   GENDER
When referring to any person, "he," "his," and "him" may also be read as "she," "her," and "hers."

---

* Words and phrases defined in Article 10 of this code and in the Hampstead-Haven Code appear in initial capitals throughout these provisions.

PARA. 10.2   CHILD

A Child is a person who, because he is less than 18 years of age (or some other age established by the legislature), is presumed, in law, to be dependent and incapable of making decisions for himself.

PARA. 10.3   ADULT

An Adult is a person who, because he is 18 years or older (or some other age established by the legislature), is presumed, in law, to be independent and capable of making decisions for himself.*

PARA. 10.4   PARENT

Parents are Adults who have the right and responsibility, in law, to make decisions for their Child. Persons become the Parents of a Child by

     a. Initial assignment at the birth of their Child; or
     b. Court decree following the request of either or both separating Parents; or
     c. Adoption; or
     d. Being designated Foster Parents with Tenure.

PARA. 10.5   LONGTIME CARETAKER

A Longtime Caretaker is an Adult with whom a Child has been placed and who has continuously cared for this Child for

     a. A period of 1 or more years if the Child was

---

* Nonadults who produce a child may become emancipated and treated as Adults in law so long as they remain responsible for the care of their child.

less than 3 years old at the time of placement; *or*

b. A period of 2 or more years if the Child was 3 years old or older at the time of placement.

Longtime Caretakers are presumed to be Parents.

PARA. 10.6   PARENTAL AUTONOMY

Parental Autonomy is the right of Parents to raise their Children as they think best, in accordance with their own notions of child rearing. The Child's physical and mental development, including the development of mutual attachments between Parent and Child, requires family privacy, free from outside control or coercive intervention by the state.

PARA. 10.7   FAMILY INTEGRITY

Family Integrity incorporates the Parents' right to Autonomy, a Child's right to Autonomous Parents, and family privacy.

PARA. 10.8   LEAST DETRIMENTAL AVAILABLE ALTERNATIVE

The Least Detrimental Available Alternative is that Child Placement and procedure for Child Placement which maximizes, in accord with the Child's Sense of Time, the Child's opportunity for being wanted and for maintaining on a continuous, unconditional, and permanent basis a relationship with at least one Adult who is or will become the Child's Psychological Parent.[1]

PARA. 10.9   TEMPORARY FOSTER CARE PLACEMENT

A Temporary Foster Care Placement occurs when, with the consent of his Parents, or, in the absence of their consent after a full hearing, a Child is placed under the temporary care of Adults who are not his Parents. The goal of Temporary Foster Care is to maintain the Child's ties to his Parents and to assure their reunion as quickly as possible. Foster Care Placement ceases to be Temporary when the Child's Foster Parents become his Longtime Caretakers.

PARA. 10.10   EMERGENCY PLACEMENT

An Emergency Placement occurs when, because a Child is reasonably believed to be threatened with imminent risk of death or serious bodily harm, the state is authorized to place him under care and custody pending a hearing to determine whether there is a Ground for Intervention.

PARA. 10.11   PERMANENT PLACEMENT

A Permanent Placement is any Placement of a Child that is neither a Temporary Foster Care Placement nor an Emergency Placement. Assignments by birth certificate, by custody decree, by adoption, and by the acquisition of Longtime Caretaker are Permanent Placements. Permanent Placements insulate Adult and Child from intrusion by former Parents or by the state except as authorized by a Ground for Intervention.

PARA. 10.12   FOSTER CARE WITH TENURE

Foster Care with Tenure is the Permanent Placement of a Child with Adults who wish to care for him but who cannot or choose not to adopt him.

PARA. 10.13   GROUND FOR INTERVENTION
A Ground for Intervention defines circumstances under which the state is authorized to investigate and/or to modify or terminate the legal relationship between a Child and his Parents.
The goal of intervention is to maintain, reestablish, or establish for the Child a Permanent Placement in a family with Autonomous Parents.

PARA. 10.14   VIOLATION OF FAMILY INTEGRITY
A Violation of Family Integrity occurs when the state coercively intrudes between Parent and Child except as authorized by a Ground for Intervention.

PARA. 10.15   CHILD ABUSE BY THE STATE
Child Abuse by the State occurs when there has been a Violation of Family Integrity or when an agent of the state returns a Child to his Parent after an Adjudication that serious bodily injury was inflicted on him by that Parent.

ARTICLE 20.   STAGES OF INTERVENTION

PARA. 20.1   INVOCATION
The Child Placement process may be invoked by
    a. The state's investigating a particular Child's circumstances, but only if it has a reasonable basis for believing that a Ground for Intervention might exist.
    b. The state's charging a Ground for Intervention if it has probable cause for believing

that a Ground for Intervention can be established *and* that a less detrimental alternative can be provided for the Child.

c. A Parent's request for the court to make a Disposition. Such a request eliminates the need for an Adjudication.

PARA. 20.2 ADJUDICATION

Following a charge of a Ground for Intervention, the court shall provide Parents with an opportunity to be heard both on their own behalf and as representatives of the Child. The court shall determine whether the state has established a Ground for Intervention. If no Ground for Intervention has been established, the court shall dismiss the action.

PARA. 20.3 DISPOSITION

Following an Adjudication that a Ground for Intervention exists, or following a request by a Parent for a Disposition, the court may appoint independent counsel for the Child, and all the parties shall have the opportunity to be heard as to which Disposition they believe to be in the Child's best interest. The court shall order the Least Detrimental Available Placement.

PARA. 20.4 DEGREE OF INTERVENTION

The degree of coercive intrusion on Family Integrity at Invocation, Adjudication, and Disposition shall be no greater than necessary. Investigations, hearings, trials and appeals shall be conducted as rapidly as is consistent with responsible decision-making and in accord with the specific Child's Sense of Time.[2]

ARTICLE 30.   GROUNDS FOR INTERVENTION

The Grounds for Intervention are:

PARA. 30.1   Refusal of Parents to comply with generally applicable immunization, education, and labor laws so far as they apply to their Children.

PARA. 30.2   Commission by a Child of an offense which would be criminal if committed by an Adult.

PARA. 30.3   The request by either or both separating Parents (whether married to each other or not) for the court to determine custody. The court is authorized to determine the Disposition only of those Children about whose custody their Parents do not agree.

PARA. 30.4   The request by a Parent for the court to terminate that Parent's legal relationship to his Child. If only one of two Parents petitions for a termination of rights, the Child's custody shall automatically remain with the other Parent.

PARA. 30.5   The death or absence of both Parents or the only Parent, when coupled with their failure to make provision for their Child's custody and care.

PARA. 30.6   A Parent's conviction, or acquittal by reason of insanity, of a sexual offense against
his Child.

PARA. 30.7   Serious bodily injury inflicted by Parents
upon their Child, or an attempt to inflict
such injury, or the repeated failure of
Parents to prevent their Child from suffering such injury.

PARA. 30.8   The refusal by Parents to authorize medical care for their Child when
a.   Medical experts agree that treatment
is nonexperimental and appropriate for
the Child; *and*
b.   Denial of that treatment will result in
the Child's death; *and*
c.   The treatment can reasonably be expected to result in a chance for the
Child to have normal healthy growth
or a life worth living.

PARA. 30.9   The request by a Child's Longtime Caretakers to become his Parents, or their refusal to relinquish him to his Parents or to
a state agency. If it is established that there
are Longtime Caretakers who request to
become a Child's Parents or refuse to relinquish him to his Parents or to a state
agency, the Longtime Caretakers shall, except as provided below, be designated as
adoptive Parents, or, if they are unwilling

or unable to adopt, as Foster Parents with Tenure.

Such Dispositions shall be automatic unless qualified absent Parents demand a Disposition hearing. Absent Parents are qualified to demand such a hearing only if

a. The Child was over 5 years old at the time of Placement with the Longtime Caretakers and had been in the continuous care and control of his Parents for not less than the 3 preceding years; *and*

b. The Child had not been separated from the absent Parents because they inflicted or attempted to inflict serious bodily injury upon him or were convicted, or acquitted by reason of insanity, of a sexual offense against him.

At such a hearing the court shall determine whether the absent Parents are still Psychological Parents [3] of the Child, and whether his return to them would provide the least detrimental alternative. If so, the Child shall be returned to them. If not, the Longtime Caretakers shall be designated as his adoptive Parents or as Foster Parents with Tenure.

PARA. 30.10   The establishment of any of the above Grounds for modifying or terminating Parent-Child relationships, or an Emergency Placement pending Adjudication, or a request by Parents who are unable to obtain legal assistance for their Child authorizes court appointment of counsel to represent the Child's interests.[4]

ARTICLE 40. ACCOUNTABILITY

PARA. 40.0   IMMUNITY FROM LIABILITY

Governmental immunity is not a defense to a charge that an agent of the state has violated Family Integrity or has committed Child Abuse.

Notes

CHAPTER 1: THE PROBLEM AND OUR CONVICTIONS

1. J. Goldstein, A. Freud, and A. J. Solnit, *Beyond the Best Interests of the Child* (New York: Free Press, 1973, p. 8) (hereinafter cited as *Beyond the Best Interests of the Child*).

2. *Beyond the Best Interests of the Child* (p. 153, n. 11):

   > In Juvenile delinquency proceedings involving violent conduct, even if the law were to make society's immediate safety the primary goal, we would argue that within that ambit the least detrimental alternative placement should be selected for the child.

   And see Part Two, Introduction and footnotes, pp. 28–29, 213–16.

3. *Beyond the Best Interests of the Child* (pp. 31, 40, 49).

4. *Beyond the Best Interests of the Child* (p. 53). For a discussion of this standard see *ibid.* (pp. 53–64).

5. While everyone may have different standards for what it means to shoulder the responsibilities of "being adult," and we have our own personal criteria for evaluating who lives up to them, the law in a secular so-

ciety looks only to an objective criterion—chronological age—to determine who shall have the rights and responsibilities of being an "adult." These privileges may be forfeited by certain failures, notably criminal behavior, but to have reached the statutory age in law *is* to be an adult. Concerning the distinction between being "adult" and being "an adult," see Joseph Goldstein, On Being Adult and Being An Adult in Secular Law (*Daedalus*, 105: 69–87, 1976).

6. Jeremy Bentham, *Theory of Legislation* (Boston: Weeks, Jordan, 1840, Vol. I, p. 248).

7. Sigmund Freud, Inhibitions, Symptoms and Anxiety [1926]. *Standard Edition*, 20:154–55 (London: Hogarth Press, 1959).

8. See J. Bowlby, *Maternal Care and Mental Health* (Geneva: World Health Organization, Monogr. Series No. 2, 1952); Alice Balint, *The Early Years of Life* (New York: Basic Books, 1954); S. Ritvo and A. J. Solnit, Influences of Early Mother-Child Interaction on Identification Processes. In *The Psychoanalytic Study of the Child*, 13:64–85 (New York: International Universities Press, 1958); Erik H. Erikson, *Identity and the Life Cycle* (New York: International Universities Press, *Psychol. Issues,* Monogr. 1, 1959); S. Ritvo and A. J. Solnit, The Relationship of Early Ego Identifications to Superego Formation (*Int. J. Psycho-Anal.,* 41:295–300, 1960); Mary D. Ainsworth, R. G. Andry, Robert G. Harlow, S. Lebovici, Margaret Mead, Dane G. Prugh, and Barbara Wootton, *Deprivation of Maternal Care* (Geneva: World Health Organization, Public Health Papers 14, 1962); Anna Freud, The Theory

of the Parent-Infant Relationship [1962]. In *The Writings of Anna Freud* 5:187–93 (New York: International Universities Press, 1969); *idem,* The Emotional and Social Development of Young Children [1962] (*ibid.,* pp. 336–51); *idem, Normality and Pathology in Childhood* (*ibid.,* Vol. 6, 1965); René A. Spitz (in collaboration with W. Godfrey Cobliner), *The First Year of Life* (New York: International Universities Press, 1965); Milton J. E. Senn and A. J. Solnit, *Problems in Child Behavior and Development* (Philadelphia: Lea & Febiger, 1968); Margaret S. Mahler, Fred Pine, and Anni Bergman, *The Psychological Birth of the Human Infant* (New York: Basic Books, 1975).

9. See Anna Freud, Adolescence [1958]. In *The Writings of Anna Freud* 5:136–66 (*supra,* 1969); Peter Blos, *On Adolescence* (New York: Free Press, 1962); *idem,* The Second Individuation Process of Adolescence. In *The Psychoanalytic Study of the Child,* 22:162–86 (New York: International Universities Press, 1967); *idem,* The Genealogy of the Ego Ideal. In *The Psychoanalytic Study of the Child,* 29:43–68. (New Haven: Yale University Press, 1974); Helene Deutsch, *Selected Problems of Adolescence* (New York: International Universities Press, *The Psychoanalytic Study of the Child Monogr. Series* 3, 1967); Erik H. Erikson, The Concept of Ego Identity; and The Problem of Ego Identity. In *The Psychology of Adolescence,* ed. Aaron H. Esman (New York: International Universities Press, 1975, pp. 178–92, 318–46).

10. But see Michael Rutter, *Maternal Deprivation Reassessed* (Middlesex, England: Penguin Books, 1972);

Richard B. Kearsley, Philip R. Zelazo, Jerome Kagan, and Rebecca Hartmann, Separation Protest in Day-Care and Home-Reared Infants (*Pediatrics,* 55:171–74, 1975; Ann M. Clarke and A. C. B. Clarke, *Early Experience: Myth and Evidence* (New York: Free Press, 1976); Barbara Tizard, *Adoption: A Second Chance* (London: Open Books, 1977); and Jerome Kagan, Richard B. Kearsley, and Philip R. Zelazo, *Infancy: Its Place in Human Development* (Cambridge, Mass.: Harvard University Press, 1978).

These and other behavioral psychologists emphasize the resilience of cognitive functions, claiming that intellectual performance is relatively resistant to differing social environmental stimuli and deprivation in early childhood. Building their theory of child development not on emotional but mainly on cognitive or group social assessments, they question the detrimental impact on a young child of being separated from or not having a primary psychological parent. However, their reliance on the resilience of cognitive function as evidence of the child's well-being is simplistic.

Psychoanalytic theory, along with Piaget's work on cognitive development, recognizes that maturational capacities and social environmental experiences are dynamically involved in the child's developmental capabilities and progression; and that our limited ability to make long-term predictions contradicts the assumption that we can make estimates about long-term resilience based mainly on cognitive assessments. Such an assumption ignores the complexities of nature and nurture and artificially reduces social, emotional, and intellectual functioning to that in which cognitive measurements are the main index of sound development. In turn, this reductionist assumption has led to false ex-

pectations that the child's cognitive resilience will protect him from and enable him to overcome earlier
environmental deprivations, disruptions, and losses.
Such misplaced expectations have encouraged parents
and policy makers to be too undemanding about standards of day care or alternate arrangements for young
children.

Scientific findings reinforce our conviction that
young children, as well as adults, deserve a decent
quality of life; and that it is essential to provide them
with a continuity of both affectionate (emotional) care
and cognitive stimulation. Only such care can prepare
them to move ahead soundly to the next phase of their
development. See Jean Piaget, *The Construction of Reality in the Child* [1937] (New York: Ballantine
Books, 1964); A. Freud and D. Burlingham, *Infants
Without Families* [1944]. In *The Writings of Anna
Freud*, 3:543–664 (*supra*, 1973); E. H. Erikson, *Childhood and Society* (New York: Norton, 1950); R. W.
Coleman and S. Provence, Environmental Retardation
(Hospitalism) in Infants Living in Families (*Pediat-
rics*, 19:285–92, 1957); S. Provence and R. C. Lipton,
Infants in Institutions (New York: International Uni-
versities Press, 1962); D. G. Prugh and R. G. Harlow,
"Masked Deprivation" in Infants and Young Children.
In *Deprivation of Maternal Care* (Geneva: World
Health Organization, Public Health Papers, No. 14,
1962); L. J. Yarrow, Separation from Parents during
Early Childhood. In *Review of Child Development Re-
search*, ed. M. L. Hoffman and L. W. Hoffman (New
York: Russell Sage Foundation, Vol. 1, 1964); C. M.
Heinicke and I. Westheimer, *Brief Separations* (New
York: International Universities Press, 1965); M. F.
Leonard, J. P. Rhymes, and A. J. Solnit, Failure to

Thrive in Infants (*Amer. J. Dis. Child.*, 111:600–12, 1966); James Robertson and Joyce Robertson, *Young Children in Brief Separation*, Films, 1: *Kate, Aged Two Years Five Months in Fostercare for Twenty-Seven Days;* 2: *Jane, Aged Seventeen Months in Fostercare for Ten Days;* 3: *John, Aged Seventeen Months Nine Days in a Residential Nursery* (London: Tavistock Child Development Research Unit, 1967–68); J. Bowlby, *Attachment and Loss*, Vol. 1: *Attachment;* Vol. 2: *Separation* (New York: Basic Books, 1969, 1973); S. Provence, A Clinician's View of Affect Development in Infancy. In *The Development of Affect*, ed. M. Lewis and L. A. Rosenblum (New York: Plenum Publishing Corp., 1978, pp. 293–307); Gale E. Inoff, Charles F. Halverson, Jr., Martin G. Allen, and Donald J. Cohen, Pathways between Constitution and Competence during the First Five Years of Life (*Develpm. Psychobiol.*, 1979, in press).

11. This is not unlike what Chafee had in mind when he said that "the First Amendment and other parts of the law erect a fence inside which men can talk. The lawmakers, legislators and officials stay on the outside of that fence." Zechariah Chafee, Jr., *The Blessings of Liberty* (Philadelphia: J. B. Lippincott, 1956, p. 108).

12. Mr. Justice Harlan dissenting in *Poe* v. *Ullman*, 367 U.S. 497, 551–52, (1961)—later relied upon in his concurrence in *Griswold* v. *Connecticut*, 381 U.S. 479, 499–500 (1965).

13. See, e.g., *Stanley* v. *Illinois*, 405 U.S. 645 (1972) and *Smith* v. *Organization of Foster Families*, 431 U.S. 816, 843–45 (1977), where the Court said:

A biological relationship is not present in the case of the usual foster family. But biological relationships are not exclusive determination of the existence of a family. The basic foundation of the family in our society, the marriage relationship, is of course not a matter of blood relation. . . .

[T]he importance of the familial relationship, to the individuals involved and to the society, stems from the emotional attachments that derive from the intimacy of daily association, and from the role it plays in 'promot[ing] a way of life' through the instruction of children, *Wisconsin* v. *Yoder,* 406 U.S. 205, 231–33 (1972), as well as from the fact of blood relationship. No one would seriously dispute that a deeply loving and interdependent relationship between an adult and a child in his or her care may exist even in the absence of a blood relationship. At least where a child has been placed in foster care as an infant, has never known his natural parents, and has remained continuously for several years in the care of the same foster parents, it is natural that the foster family should hold the same place in the emotional life of the foster child, and fulfill the same socializing functions as a natural family. For this reason we cannot dismiss the foster family as a mere collection of unrelated individuals.

Mr. Justice Powell, in striking down a zoning ordinance which made it unlawful for a mother, son, and two grandchildren to occupy the same dwelling as a family unit in *Moore* v. *City of East Cleveland, Ohio,*

431 U.S. 494 (1977), observed for the United States Supreme Court:

> Our decisions establish that the Constitution protects the sanctity of the family precisely because the institution of the family is deeply rooted in this Nation's history and tradition. It is through the family that we inculcate and pass down many of our most cherished values, moral and cultural.
>
> Ours is by no means a tradition limited to respect for the bonds uniting the members of the nuclear family. The tradition of uncles, aunts, cousins, and especially grandparents sharing a household along with parents and children has roots equally venerable and equally deserving of constitutional recognition. Over the years millions of our citizens have grown up in just such an environment, and most, surely, have profited from it. Even if conditions of modern society have brought about a decline in extended family households, they have not erased the accumulated wisdom of civilization, gained over the centuries and honored throughout our history, that supports a larger conception of the family. Out of choice, necessity, or a sense of family responsibility, it has been common for close relatives to draw together and participate in the duties and the satisfactions of a common home. . . . Especially in times of adversity, such as the death of a spouse or economic need, the broader family has tended to come together for mutual sustenance and to maintain or rebuild a secure home life [*id.* at 503–05].

Mr. Justice Brennan, with whom Mr. Justice Marshall joined, concurred:

> The Constitution cannot be interpreted . . . to tolerate the imposition by government upon the rest of us of white suburbia's preference in patterns of family living. . . .
>
> The "extended" form is especially familiar among black families. We may suppose that this reflects the truism that black citizens, like generations of white immigrants before them, have been victims of economic and other disadvantages that would worsen if they were compelled to abandon extended, for nuclear, living patterns [*id.* at 508–09].

14. See also *Commonwealth ex rel. Children's Aid Society v. Gard*, 362 Pa. 85, 97, 66 A.2d 300, 306 (1949), an opinion recognizing that ties of blood may weaken over time:

> To take this nearly 65 months old girl . . . away from the only parents she has known since she was an infant of eighteen months would be exactly the same in its effect on her and on the man and woman who have stood in a parental relationship to her for nearly four years as would the separation of any well cared for child from its own parents. Nothing could be more cruel than the forceable separation of a child from either its real or foster parents by whom it has been lovingly cared for and to whom it is bound by strong ties of affection; to a child it is equally cruel whether the separation is brought about by "kidnapping" or by legal process.

15. See Chapter 4, note 12 on the meaning of object constancy; and Chapter 4, note 14 concerning the Michigan Legislature's decision to create a statutory presumption in favor of "custodial family units" in custody proceedings, even if it means depriving biological parents of their child.

16. For discussion of the limitations of law in child placement, see *Beyond the Best Interests of the Child* (pp. 49–52).

17. Parents must not only have certain ways of guiding by prohibition and permission; they must also be able to represent to the child a deep, an almost somatic conviction that there is a meaning to what they are doing. In this sense a traditional system of child care can be said to be a factor making for trust, even where certain items of that tradition, taken singly, may seem unnecessarily cruel. Here much depends on whether such items are inflicted on the child by the parent in the firm belief that this is the only way to do things or whether the parent misuses his administration of the baby or the child in order to work off anger, alleviate fear or win an argument, with the child or with somebody else (mother, husband, doctor, or priest). The latter kind of situation we shall refer to as the parental *exploitation of the inequality* between adult and child. See Erik H. Erikson, Growth and Crises of the "Healthy Personality." In *Personality in Nature, Society, and Culture*, ed. C. Kluckhohn, H. A. Murray, and D. M. Schneider (New York: Alfred A. Knopf, 1953, pp. 185–225).

18. Orphanages, which at one time seemed to be a feasible

alternative to the family, proved thoroughly disappointing as a solution for the uprooted child. Although offering physical care and survival, they usually failed to grant their inmates relationships which are necessary for the development of self-esteem, of internal mechanisms for impulse control, and of the capacity for maintaining meaningful personal relationships.

Foster care does hold out the promise of returning to the child the advantages of the lost family situation, but it has also been found seriously wanting. Foster care policy seems to discourage the attachments that it ought to promote. It discards the idea of guaranteed continuity, it restricts the autonomy of the foster parents by means of administrative regulations, and it discourages rather than encourages the natural proprietary responses of the foster parents that can and should be part and parcel of the adults' full involvement with the child in their care. See Chapter 4, p. 50 and note 15.

CHAPTER 2:   THE FRAMEWORK

1. Talk by E. James Anthony, "A Mind that Lost Itself: A Prospective Study of Mental Decompensation from Birth to Breakdown," at the Yale Child Study Center in New Haven, Connecticut (April 9, 1977).

2. U.S. CONST. amend. IV.

3. Interventions to establish and to correct violations of these provisions are perceived and explained not exclusively in terms of *parens patriae* or the child's best interests, but rather in terms of "reasonable and proper exercises of police power"—of "compelling state inter-

ests" in protecting employment opportunities for adults and in assuring for the state a minimally literate and healthy citizenry.

With regard to vaccination, see, e.g., *Jacobson* v. *Massachusetts*, 197 U.S. 11, 26 (1905), upholding the constitutionality of a compulsory smallpox vaccination law:

> [T]he liberty secured by the Constitution of the United States to every person within its jurisdiction does not import an absolute right in each person to be, at all times and in all circumstances, wholly freed from restraint. There are manifold restraints to which every person is necessarily subject for the common good.

See generally *Wisconsin* v. *Yoder,* 406 U.S. 205 (1972), and R. H. Mnookin, *Child, Family and State* (Boston: Little, Brown, 1978).

4. Alexander M. Bickel, *The Least Dangerous Branch* (Indianapolis: Bobbs-Merrill, 1962, p. 151).

See also Chapter 5, note 34, and *Bowers* v. *State,* 389 A. 2d 341, 349 (Md. Ct. App. 1978):

> [In amending the child abuse statute to impose liability on a parent or custodian who causes his child or ward to sustain physical injury "as a result of cruel or inhumane treatment or as a result of other malicious acts" the Maryland legislature employed terminology] sufficiently explicit to survive even strict scrutiny under the Due Process Clause. First, it meets the requirement of notice, such that persons of common intelligence need not guess at its meaning or speculate as to its application. . . . Par-

ents of ordinary intelligence are made aware
that they do not subject themselves to the
statute by merely engaging in corporal discipline for the purpose of punishment or correc-
tion. Only when the line is crossed and physical
injury is intentionally and maliciously or cruelly
inflicted does criminal responsibility attach. In
short, the statute provides fair warning; it sets
no trap for the unwary or innocent parent.
[This is so even though they may not know, at the
time they act, that their conduct is prohibited.]
Similarly, the statute neither invites selective or
discriminatory application by law enforcement
authorities nor confers impermissible discretion
upon judges and juries. The language . . . draws
for the benefit of police officers, prosecutors and
triers of fact reasonably clear lines between the
kinds of parentally inflicted corporal punishment that are criminal and those that are not.
Police, court and jury are precluded from re-
acting to nothing more than their own subjective ideas of child discipline.

See Chapter 5, note 22 and accompanying text.
On the absence of fair warning and consequently
of power restraint in child welfare legislation in England see Lord Justice Sachs in *Hewer* v. *Bryant* [1970]
1 Q.B. 357, 371 (1969):

In the end, so far as comprehensibility . . . is
concerned, one finds that this voluminous and
well-intentioned legislation has created a bureau-
crat's paradise and a citizen's nightmare.

See also J. M. Eekelaar, What Are Parental Rights? 89
L. Quart. Rev., 210 (1973).

5. Sanford N. Katz, Melba McGrath, and Ruth-Arlene Howe, *Child Neglect Laws in America* (American Bar Association Section on Family Law, 1976).

6. Another possibly useful way to characterize the difference between the well-specified state aims and interventions of the first form and the fuzzy ones of the second is in terms of the kind of intervention that is authorized. The first is usually, though certainly not always, associated with one-shot or one-issue interventions (a vaccination); the second is more likely to be accompanied by continuing intrusions (custody, foster care). The first seems more of a response to an acute problem; the second, to what is perceived as a chronic problem. See Note, *Parens Patriae* and Statutory Vagueness in the Juvenile Court, 82 *Yale L. J.*, 745 (1973) (arguing that despite the substantial historic immunity of juvenile statutes containing "omnibus clauses" with broad definitions of "delinquency," such statutes should be struck down as unconstitutionally vague). See also Note, The Void-For-Vagueness Doctrine in the Supreme Court, 109 *U. Pa. L. Rev.*, 67 (1960).

7. B. D. Underwood, The Thumb on the Scales of Justice: Burdens of Persuasion in Criminal Cases, 86 *Yale L. J.*, 1299, 1300–01 (1977):

    > [A] factual issue is close for decision if the two sides are in equipoise; in that event, neither side can be said to have a preponderance of evidence and therefore the party with the burden loses.

8. See Miloran Djilas, *The Unperfect Society* (New York: Harcourt, Brace & World, 1969, pp. 4–5):

> [S]ociety cannot be perfect. Men must hold both ideas and ideals, but they should not regard these as being wholly realizable. We need to comprehend the nature of utopianism. Utopianism, once it achieves power, becomes dogmatic, and it can quite readily create human suffering in the name and in the cause of its own scientism and idealism. To speak of society as imperfect may seem to imply that it *can* be perfect, which in truth it cannot. The task for contemporary man is to accept the reality that society is unperfect, but also to understand that humanist, humanitarian dreams and visions are necessary in order to reform society, in order to improve and advance it.

9. *Beyond the Best Interests of the Child* (p. 66, footnote).

10. On a child's sense of time and the detriment that results from separation and the uncertainty that accompanies delay in determining who are his parents, see Chapter 4 and *Beyond the Best Interests of the Child* (pp. 40–49).

    For a discussion of the suspended judgment notion in another context, see J. Goldstein, The *Brawner* Rule—Why? Or No More Nonsense on Non Sense in the Criminal Law, Please! 1973 *Wash. U. L. Quart.*, 126, 131 (1973).

11. The Alaskan Supreme Court has promulgated special

rules of procedure which identify and distinguish these three stages. Rule 8(d) of the Alaska Rules of Children's Procedure requires that invocation be by means of a petition which includes, *inter alia*, a "brief statement of the facts which bring the child within the court's child jurisdiction." The rule specifically provides that for the purposes of such a petition, "mere conclusions or the reiteration of statutory language are not sufficient." Rule 12(a) divides the child hearing into an adjudicative phase and a dispositive phase and then describes the two phases as follows:

> (1) *Adjudicative Phase.* The adjudicative phase determines the issue of delinquency or dependency, or both, or need of supervision, according to allegations of the petition for adjudication. These issues may be determined either by the admission or confession of the party or by the taking of evidence.
>
> (2) *Dispositive Phase.* The dispositive phase consists of the measures taken and the orders issued by the court with respect to the child or his parents, guardian, or custodian, designed to correct any undesirable situation found in the adjudicative phase.

For an illustration of the manner in which Alaska courts consider each stage of decision separately, see *Matter of S.D., Jr.*, 549 P.2d 1190 (Alaska 1976).

12. See *Beyond the Best Interests of the Child* (pp. 38–39), and Epilogue in New Edition concerning our opposition to forced visitation and how our position squares with our concerns for continuity.

PART TWO: GROUNDS FOR INTERVENTION—
INTRODUCTION

1. Institute of Judicial Administration/American Bar Association Joint Commission on Juvenile Justice Standards, *Standards Relating to Noncriminal Misbehavior* (Cambridge, Mass.: Ballinger Publishing Co., 1977, § 1.1, at p. 35).

2. See Note, Ungovernability: The Unjustifiable Jurisdiction, 83 *Yale L. J.*, 1383 (1974), and American Bar Association Joint Commission on Juvenile Justice Standards, *Standards Relating to Noncriminal Misbehavior* (*supra*):

> As the California legislature noted, "Not a single shred of evidence exists to indicate that any significant number of [beyond control children] have benefited [by juvenile court intervention]. In fact, what evidence does exist points to the contrary." Report of the California Assembly Interim Committee on Criminal Procedure, *Juvenile Court Processes* 7 (1971) [*id.* at 3].
>
> Even in cases where there is no order of institutional commitment, the juvenile court's status offense jurisdiction is not apt. A fourteen-year-old's being lazy, failing to do assigned chores, buying a sandwich at a place her mother had told her not to go to, and "being a disruptive influence" should not support secure interim custody, judicial intervention, or official probation supervision, sustained in *In re Walker*, 14 N.C. App. 356, 188 S.E.2d 731 (1972), *aff'd* 282 N.C. 28, 191 S.E.2d 702 (1972) [*id.* at 7].

A further problem is that the ungovernability statutes are almost invariably impermissibly vague in wording and overbroad in scope. Such language as that extending jurisdiction over a child "who is in danger, from any cause, of leading an idle, dissolute or immoral life," Cal. Welf. & Inst'ns Code §601 (West Supp. 1975) [but note that this language has been stricken from the California statute by A.B. 432, signed by the governor 7/7/75, effective 1/1/76]; or who is "ungovernable," D.C. Code Ann. §16–2301 (Supp. 1973); or who is "growing up in idleness and crime," see, *e.g.,* Wyo. Stat. Ann. §14-41 (Supp. 1973), falls far short of the specificity that would allow a minor to determine what behavior fell within the prohibitions of the statute and what lay without. Given the overbreadth of these statutes, every child in the United States could theoretically be made out to be a status offender. How many children have not disobeyed their parents at least twice? [*id.* at 8].

The statutes conferring juvenile court jurisdiction over ungovernable youth are arguably infected with constitutional infirmity on yet another basis: infringement of the equal protection clause. Virtually without exception, the defined class—children—is underinclusive and hence suspect because the child is subject to sanction and the parent, who shares responsibility for the child's behavior, is untouched by the law. Sidman, "The Massachusetts Stubborn Child Law: Law and Order in the Home," 6 *Fam. L.Q.* 33, 49–56 (1972); see, *e.g., State* v.

In Interest of S.M.G., 313 So. 2d 761 (Fla. Sup. Ct. 1975) (juvenile court lacks jurisdiction to order the parent of a delinquent child to participate in the child's rehabilitative program).

Finally, the Supreme Court of the U.S. has ruled that it is constitutionally impermissible to impose sanctions on a status in the case of an adult, *Robinson* v. *California,* 370 U.S. 660 (1972). Yet, . . . that is what the juvenile court's status offense jurisdiction does with respect to unruly children.

The jurisdiction over unruly children is thus a kind of moral thumbscrew by which we seek to demand of our communities' children a greater and more exacting adherence to desired norms than we are willing to impose upon ourselves [*id.* at 11].

3.   As a replacement for juvenile delinquency and ungovernability provisions, we propose (in Appendix II, para. 30.2) the following as a ground for intervention:

Commission by a Child of an offense which would be criminal if committed by an Adult.

4.   See *Beyond the Best Interests of the Child* (p. 153, n. 11). Further, we share these observations in E. H. Erikson, *Identity: Youth and Crisis* (New York: Norton, 1968, p. 132):

Youth after youth, bewildered by the incapacity to assume a role forced on him by the inexorable standardization of American adolescence, runs away in one form or another, dropping out of school, leaving jobs, staying out all night, or withdrawing into bizarre and inaccessible moods. Once "delinquent," his greatest need and often his only salvation is the refusal on the part of older friends, advisers, and judiciary personnel to type him further by pat diagnoses and social judgments which ignore the special dynamic conditions of adolescence.

5. For a brief discussion of these requirements, see Chapter 2, p. 16.

CHAPTER 3:   PARENTAL REQUESTS FOR THE STATE TO PLACE THE CHILD

1. See *Velasquez* v. *Jankowski*, 5 F.L.R. 2088, 2089 (N.Y. Sup. Ct. 1978), in which even a natural parent, after the death of his ex-spouse, is denied custody because it would require separating two half sisters who went to live with their aunt and uncle following their mother's death. The court said:

> What does exist in the matter at bar . . . upon which the court makes its determination, is that "rare, extraordinary circumstance which could drastically affect the welfare of the child. . . ." I cannot and will not award the older child, Mary, to the petitioner. If I were to award Frances [petitioner's child], there would be perforce, a separation of these two sisters that would be disastrous to both of them. I was able to discern the fear on their faces and voices at the prospect of their separation. It would be cruel and heartless to both of these girls to separate them and a separation would be de-

structive to their future. Courts should be reluctant to permit separate custody of siblings
and separations between siblings is frowned
upon [cases omitted]. "Young brothers and sisters need each other's strengths and association
in their everyday and often common experiences,
and to separate them unnecessarily, is likely to
be traumatic and harmful." (*Obey* v. *Degling,*
36 N.Y.2d 768)

2. *Prince* v. *Massachusetts,* 321 U.S. 158, 166 (1944). And
    see *Moore* v. *City of East Cleveland,* 431 U.S. 494, 499
    (1977) and cases cited therein. See also *Kilgrow* v. *Kil-
    grow,* 107 So.2d 885 (Ala. 1959), holding that courts
    have no jurisdiction to settle differences of opinion be-
    tween parents as to what is best for their child when
    the parents and child are living together as a family
    group.

3. See generally *Beyond the Best Interests of the Child*
    (pp. 37–39, 46–47, 49–52).

4. Even if separating parents are in agreement about cus-
    tody, courts generally have the final say. In England,
    for example, the Matrimonial Causes Act 1973, s.41,
    and Form 2 of the Matrimonial Causes Rules 1973 pro-
    vides "with regard to the custody . . . the divorce . . .
    decree cannot be made absolute *until the court has
    declared itself satisfied with the arrangements proposed
    for the care of the children or that no more satisfactory
    arrangements can be made*" (O. Stone, *Family Law.*
    London: Macmillan Press, 1977, pp. 19–20).

    The following from the Uniform Marriage and

Divorce Act §403 (Second Tent. Draft 1970) was rejected by drafting committee of National Conference of Commissioners on Uniform State Laws:

> Unless the court finds that the child's physical health or emotional stability will be significantly jeopardized by the award the court shall find that the best interest of the child will be served by awarding custody:
>
> (a) to the person selected by the parents. . . .

And see R. H. Mnookin, *Child, Family and State* (Boston: Little, Brown, 1978, pp. 473–74).

5. See discussion of *Comerford* v. *Cherry,* 100 So. 2d 385 (Fla. 1958), in Chapter 5, pp. 60–61.

6. *State ex rel. Scarpetta* v. *Spence-Chapin Adoption Service,* 28 N.Y.2d 185, 192, 269 N.E.2d 787, 791, *cert. denied,* 404 U.S. 805 (1971).

7. See, e.g., Iowa Code Ann. §222.41 (1969) which provided that the juvenile court may upon petition "terminate the relationships between parent and child:

> "1. With the written consent of parents who for *good cause* desire to terminate the parent-child relationship (emphasis supplied)."

This provision was repealed in 1976 and replaced by Iowa Code Ann. §600A.5 (1.a) (1978 Pocket Part) which eliminates the *for good cause* requirement but establishes a time limitation on such actions by providing that "a parent or prospective parent of the parent-child relationship" may petition "for termination of parental rights if the child . . . is born or expected to be born within one hundred eighty days of the date of petition filing."

For the apparent use of the "best interest standard" as the guide to determining "for good cause," see, e.g., Del. Code Ann. titl. 13, §§1103–1108 (1974). Section 1104 explicitly provides that parents desiring to terminate their parental rights may themselves petition the court. After a filing of a social study and report on the petition by an authorized agency or the Health and Social Services Department, the Delaware courts may, after a hearing, terminate the rights of the parents to their child, *provided that such termination is found to be in the best interests of the child*. Once a termination order has been made, the code authorizes the transfer of parental rights "to some other person or persons or authorized agency or the State Department of Health and Social Services. . . ." See §§1107–1108.

8. See *In re Janet G.*, 94 Misc.2d 133, 143–44, 403 N.Y.S. 2d 646, 652–53 (Fam. Ct. 1978), holding that the natural mother had not voluntarily, informedly, or knowingly surrendered her child for adoption:

> Waiver is suspect, and the courts are zealous in their concern with "the involuntariness or un-intelligence of a waiver" even in those cases involving only property interests. . . . *A fortiori*, where the agreement surrenders parental rights to the State, where the agreement is between the State and a minor [parent], where the minor is not aware or made aware of the legal significance of the provisions, where the minor does not know that she need not sign the papers presented to her, where the instrument is a maze of

fineprint, complex, technical provisions [the waiver is void].

9. Once a parent has voluntarily terminated his relationship to his child, he should not have standing to challenge the child's new placement. See *Matter of Maxwell*, 4 N.Y.2d. 429, 431, 151 N.E.2d 848, 850 (1958), concerning a Canadian woman who conceived a child "out of wedlock" and concealed the pregnancy from her husband. She went to a N.Y. hospital for the birth, and shortly thereafter gave up the child for adoption. Four years later, she challenged the adoption because she wanted the child brought up in the Catholic religion. The court said:

> When the appellant asserted that she did not want the baby and that she "wanted" to be done with the matter "as quickly as possible," when she did everything she could to conceal the child's very birth, and herself hid behind a false name, and when thereafter she returned to Canada and for almost a year manifested not the slightest interest in the welfare of the child, his well-being or even his continued existence, she was guilty of conduct that amounted to the abandonment found by the courts below.

10. *In re Janet G.*, 94 Misc.2d 133, 143, 403 N.Y.S.2d 646, 652 (Fam. Ct. 1978).

11. Page, The Mother's Decision (*Child Adoption*, 75:45, 52, 1974).

12. Richard A. Posner, *Economic Analysis of Law* (Boston: Little, Brown, 2nd ed., pp. 112–13).

13. Agatha Christie provides this account of her mother's being an "unwanted child":

> My mother Clara Boehmer went through unhappiness as a child. Her father, an officer in the Argyll Highlanders, was thrown from his horse and fatally injured, and my grandmother was left, a young and lovely widow with four children, at the age of 27 with nothing but her widow's pension. It was then that her elder sister, who had recently married a rich American, as his second wife, wrote to her offering to adopt one of the children and bring it up as her own.
>
> To the anxious young widow, working desperately with her needle to support and educate four children, the offer was not to be refused. Of the three boys and one girl, she selected the girl; either because it seemed to her that boys could make their way in the world while a girl needed the advantages of easy living, or because, as my mother always believed, she cared for the boys more. My mother left Jersey and came to the North of England to a strange home. I think the resentment she felt, the deep hurt at being unwanted, coloured her attitude to life. It made her distrustful of herself and suspicious of people's affection. Her aunt was a kindly woman, good-humoured and generous, but she was imperceptive of a child's feelings. My mother had all the so-called advantages of a comfortable home and a good education—what she lost and what nothing could replace was the carefree life with her brothers in *her own home*. Quite often I have seen in cor-

respondence columns inquiries from anxious
parents asking if they ought to let a child go to
others because of "the advantages she will have
which I cannot provide—such as a first-class
education." I always long to cry out: Don't let
the child go. Her own home, her own people,
love, and the security of belonging—what does
the best education in the world mean against
that?

My mother was deeply miserable in her
new life. She cried herself to sleep every night,
grew thin and pale, and at last became so ill that
her aunt called in a doctor. He was an elderly,
experienced man, and after talking to the little
girl, he went to her aunt and said:

"The child's homesick."

Her aunt was astonished and unbelieving.
"Oh no," she said. "That couldn't possibly be so.
Clara's a good quiet child, she never gives any
trouble, and she's quite happy." But the old
doctor went back to the child and talked to her
again. She had brothers, hadn't she? How
many? What were their names? And presently
the child broke down in a storm of weeping, and
the whole story came out.

Bringing out the trouble eased the strain,
but the feeling always remained of "not being
wanted." I think she held it against my grandmother until her dying day.

Agatha Christie, *An Autobiography* (Glasgow: William
Collins Sons & Co., 1977, pp. 15–16).

14. Herbert Wieder, On Being Told of Adoption (*Psycho-
     anal. Quart.*, 46:1–22, 1977).

CHAPTER 4: FAMILIAL BONDS BETWEEN
CHILDREN AND LONGTIME
CARETAKERS WHO ARE NOT
THEIR PARENTS

1. John Locke [1690], *The Second Treatise of Government* (London: J. M. Dent & Sons, 1924, p. 147):

> Nay, this [paternal] *power* so little belongs to the father by any peculiar right of nature, but only as he is guardian of his children, that when he quits his care of them, he loses his power over them, which goes along with their nourishment and education, to which it is inseparably annexed, and it belongs as much to the *foster-father* of an exposed child, as to the natural father or another; so little power does the bare *act of begetting* give a man over his issue, if all his care ends there, and this be all the title he hath to the name and authority of a father.

See Chapter 1, pp. 9–11 and *Smith* v. *Organization of Foster Families*, 431 U.S. 816 (1977).

2. Motives for fostering a child will also affect the *quality* of the caretaker's feelings for the child.

3. For a literary reflection of the "psychological child" notion see Chapter 4 in D. H. Lawrence's *The Rainbow* which describes Tom Borangwen's feelings when his adopted daughter, Anna, tells him of her plans to marry.

4. *Beyond the Best Interests of the Child* (p. 48).

5. "A wanted child is one who receives affection and nour-

ishment on a continuing basis from at least one adult and who feels that he or she is and continues to be valued by those who take care of him or her" (*Beyond the Best Interests of the Child*, p. 98, para. 10.2).

6. See, e.g., the Maria Colwell case in Appendix I and Chapter 6, The Rothman Decisions, in *Beyond the Best Interests of the Child* (pp. 71–96).

7. Amici Curiae Brief for A Group of Concerned Persons for Children at 15, *Smith* v. *Organization of Foster Families*, 431 U.S. 816 (1977).

8. See *Bennett* v. *Marrow*, 59 App. Div.2d 492, 494–496, 399 N.Y.S.2d 697, 699–700 (1977). After observing that the new hearing in the trial court extended over a 4-week period and contained the testimony of some 26 witnesses, Justice O'Connor said:

> Predicated upon his observations and findings at the 1975 hearing, the court was in a rather unique position to completely re-examine and re-evaluate the testimony of those witnesses who had testified at both hearings. In the light of his intimate knowledge of the background and history of the case, he was able to conduct a more in-depth examination of the psychiatrists, psychologists, social workers, teachers and other witnesses called by the parties. Most importantly, the court was enabled to clearly and closely observe for a second time the conduct and deportment of the principals, namely the petitioner-appellant (the natural parent), the respondent (the foster parent) and Gina Marie (the infant involved). His comments

therefore concerning the changes he found in the personality and demeanor of [8-year-old] Gina Marie become all the more significant and persuasive in view of the fact that the child [after living since infancy with her foster parents], in the intervening 15 months, had been living in the home of the petitioner, her natural mother.

The trial court, after noting that during the first hearing Gina Marie appeared to be a well-adjusted, happy child, went on to say that "the fact is that notwithstanding a period of some 15 months spent in the home of her mother, Gina Marie has not settled into the household. She does not feel comfortable there, she is not happy there. She continues unswerving in her request to be restored to the custody of her [foster mother] Mrs. Marrow."

These surface observations, while bearing some significance, are certainly not controlling; but the court's conclusions concerning the natural mother are perhaps more revealing. The court said: "To the extent that the petitioner has responded to Gina Marie's needs to be housed, to be clothed, to be fed, she could be considered to have performed adequately as a parent. But she has not begun to respond to Gina Marie's emotional needs. . . . I find that an emotional void exists between mother and daughter that shows no signs of being bridged despite the time they have resided together. This child continues to mourn the loss of her 'mother.' "

Addressing itself then to the relationship between the respondent and Gina Marie, the court gave credence to the testimony of a witness called by the Law Guardian, Dr. Sally Provence, a child psychiatrist from Yale University. Finding her to be "certainly the most impressive expert witness who appeared in this proceeding," the hearing court accepted Dr. Provence's testimony that a psychological parent-child relationship had developed between respondent and the child and the court noted that such bond "appears as strong today as when this case was first heard."

It was Dr. Provence's further testimony, in substance, that to remove the child from such a relationship would endanger the development of the child in many ways and could affect her academic success and her motivation to learn.

This testimony is all the more significant in view of the record, which discloses that in January, 1977 an intelligence test was administered to Gina Marie resulting in a score of 84, in the low-normal range, whereas in April, 1975 she had scored 113. Despite efforts to explain away this rather disturbing pattern, it seems to be, at least to some extent, buttressed by the obvious and drastic decline in the physical, mental and emotional make-up of Gina Marie.

9. See, e.g., *Beyond the Best Interests of the Child* (pp. 47–49); James and Joyce Robertson, Young Children in Brief Separation. In *The Psychoanalytic Study of the Child*, 26:264–315 (New York: Quadrangle Books, 1971, esp. pp. 264–65).

10. See *Beyond the Best Interests of the Child* (pp. 27–28, 79–80, 98) for a description of the relationship between

longtime caretakers and the child as a "common-law adoptive parent-child relationship."

11. *Village of Belle Terre* v. *Boraas,* 416 U.S. 1, 8 & n. 5 (1974), quoting *Louisville Gas* v. *Coleman,* 277 U.S. 32, 41 (1928) (dissenting opinion).

12. Object constancy is the psychoanalytic term for describing a child's capacity to retain the memory and emotional tie to his parents, and to feel their nurturing, guiding presence even when they are sources of frustration or disappointment or when they are absent. This is the second of two stages in child-parent bonding (see Chapter 1, pp. 9–11). The first stage is a need-satisfying attachment of infant to mother, an opportunity beyond the biological connection to begin reciprocal psychological relationships. Toward the end of his first year as the child becomes capable of differentiating strangers from those who care for him on an hour-to-hour basis and later himself from them, he has entered into the stage of object constancy when he can retain the emotionally charged memory of the constant or primary love objects.

 The child in his third and fourth years of life, attending an appropriate nursery school or day care program, is able to use graduated separation experiences in the service of his development. But such separation experiences in the first and second years of life could exceed the infant's capacity to hold on to the parent emotionally and cognitively, undermining his need to acquire and utilize object constancy as an essential requirement for socialization and for healthy development. Object constancy may never be achieved, or, even if achieved, would be lost in children exposed to repeated or prolonged separations or periods of emotional deprivation such as those in large institutions or in multiple foster home placements.

Object constancy is a crucial achievement, a condition for internalizing the care and attitudes of the psychological parents, enabling the child to identify with his parents in order to become increasingly active in shaping his own environment and in developing his own autonomous personality. See J. Piaget, *Play, Dreams, and Imitation in Childhood* [1945] (New York: Norton, 1951); H. Hartmann, E. Kris, and R. M. Loewenstein, Comments on the Formation of Psychic Structure. In *The Psychoanalytic Study of the Child*, 2:11–38 (New York: International Universities Press, 1946); J. D. Benjamin, Prediction and Psychopathologic Theory. In *Dynamic Psychopathology in Childhood*, ed. L. Jessner and E. Pavenstedt (New York: Grune & Stratton, pp. 6–77); P. H. Wolff, *The Developmental Psychologies of Jean Piaget and Psychoanalysis* (New York: International Universities Press, *Psychol. Issues*, Monogr. 5, 1960); M. S. Mahler, On the Significance of the Normal Separation-Individuation Phase. In *Drives, Affects, Behavior*, ed. M. Schur (New York: International Universities Press, 1965, 2:161–69); R. A. Spitz, *The First Year of Life* (*supra*); Selma Fraiberg, Libidinal Object Constancy and Mental Representation. In *The Psychoanalytic Study of the Child*, 24:9–47 (New York: International Universities Press, 1969). And see note 8 (this chapter).

13. This book's grounds for intervention and the guidelines in *Beyond the Best Interests of the Child* incorporate principles of general application that have been

distilled from psychoanalytic theory and from an extensive body of diagnostic and therapeutic work in child development. Both the grounds and the guidelines have been designed to enlarge the number of situations in which courts and other agencies of decision can determine a particular child's placement without a clinician's examination of him and of the adults seeking his custody.

The court should no longer need such examinations to confirm the fact, for example, that enforced separation of a 4-year-old from the only parent he has ever known will have serious repercussions for his development; or that the child's absent biological parent cannot, by virtue of blood ties, replace the longtime caretaker as psychological parent; or that murderous parental attacks on a child will destroy the possibility of his ever feeling safe again in the care of the assaulting parents; or that a child's capacity to develop meaningful relationships will be undermined if he is forced to maintain contact with separated parents who are not in agreement about his visits.

Clinicians will, however, continue to be called by courts and counsel to make assessments, particularly at the disposition stage. For example, courts will require an evaluation of a child's relationships to the competing adults who are entitled to claim custody under the special exception to this chapter's longtime caretaker ground. And clinical examinations may be required of persons who wish to qualify as foster or adopting parents as well as of the particular child for whom they are to be selected.

Experts are and will continue to be engaged because their training has equipped them with the interview skills to approach individual adults as well as children, because of their capacity to talk to people (particularly to children in their own language). Through such interviews and the understanding of verbal and nonverbal expressions clinicians create an intimacy in which light can be thrown on the needs and wishes of children and their parents, as well as on their strengths and weaknesses, successes and failures, and on their deviant behavior, i.e., clinicians are called on as consultants and investigators to describe and evaluate such phenomena.

What must be recognized is that the skills of these experts were developed outside the child placement process for a different purpose and under different conditions. Clinical evaluations are generally undertaken at the request of parents for their children or by adults in distress for the purpose of determining whether and what therapy or guidance would be useful for the person or persons being examined. These examinations are carried out in an atmosphere of confidentiality and without the artificial time constraints of a court or some other extrafamilial agency. Conversely, as in the case of the exception for certain older children under the longtime caretaker ground, clinical examinations in the child placement process are undertaken for the purpose of responding to questions formulated not by expert but by court, agency, or counsel about matters they consider relevant to decisions at invocation, adjudication, or disposition. Such examinations are carried out at the request of persons other than those who are examined, in an atmosphere of nonconfidentiality and under court-determined deadlines. These differences in the purposes and the conditions of examination raise not only the ethical issue to which the textual note alludes, but also questions about the transferability of the clinician's data-gathering and interpretive skills from one setting to another.

14. In the Child Custody Act of 1970, the Michigan Legislature established that a factor in determining "the best interests of the child" in custody cases is the "length of time the child has lived in a stable, satisfactory environment and the desirability of maintaining continuity" MCL 722.23 (§3c). Section 7 of the Act bars removing a child from an "established custodial environment" unless there is "clear and convincing evidence" that the change is in the best interest of the child. Without adopting statutory time periods, as we propose, the Michigan Legislature recognized the importance of *time with* the same caretaker by providing:

> The custodial environment of a child is established if over an appreciable time the child naturally looks to the custodian in such environment for guidance, discipline, the necessities of life and parental comfort [MCL 722.27 (§7c.]

For a construction of this provision, see *Bahr* v. *Bahr*, 60 Mich. App. 354, 230 N.W.2d 430 (1975).

> But see *Drummond* v. *Fulton County Dept. of Family & Children's Services*, 237 Ga. 449, 228 S.E.2d 839 (1976), *cert. denied*, 432 U.S. 905 (1977), in which foster parents were denied a petition to adopt their 2½-year-old child who had lived with them since he was 1 month old. The court said that the foster parents

> misconstrue the Georgia law in assuming that the best interests of the child rule applies to fos-

ter parents. Without this test and its focus on the child, there is no basis for recognizing any right in the "psychological parents." Since the focus in determining whether a third party is entitled to custody is on the natural parents and whether or not they have forfeited their rights or are unfit . . . any relationship between the child and his foster parents is primarily irrelevant [*id.* at 451, 228 S.E.2d at 842–43].

15. What foster care arrangements might be made for 2 to 3 weeks, possibly more, for a child between 1½ and 2½ years of age, is suggested by the work of James and Joyce Robertson. Foster "parents" would be required to discuss, whenever possible, with the infant's natural or adopted parents the child's eating, sleeping, and toilet habits and preferences, as well as the ways in which the child is comforted. The foster parents would have an opportunity to observe how the real parents talk, play, and generally handle their child. Plans might be made for the child to have with him in his foster home his own bedding, favorite toys, even a photograph of his parents and of his own room. Plans would be made, where possible, for either or both of the real parents to visit or be visited by the child. Efforts to do this would be facilitated by trying to arrange foster placements in the neighborhood of the child's real home. For the school-age child, continuity of neighborhood surroundings, for example, would facilitate maintaining ties with school and friends. The variations for trying to meet an individual child's as well as his parents' fundamental needs not to break the ties between them are countless. James and Joyce Robertson, Young Children in Brief Separation (*supra*).

16. See, e.g., *Matter of Bennett* v. *Jeffreys*, 40 N.Y.2d 543, 544 n. 1 (1976), where the court approved taking an 8-year-old child from the person with whom she was placed as a newborn baby, and leaving her with her natural mother pending determination of the mother's petition to regain custody; *Bennett* v. *Marrow*, 399 N.Y.S.2d 697 (1977), discussed in note 8, *supra; Eason* v. *Commissioner of Welfare*, 171 Conn. 630, 370 A.2d 1082 (1976), where a 6-year-old child who had lived with foster parents since shortly after birth was removed directly from school by the Welfare Commissioner and returned to the natural mother without even preparation for this separation; *Drummond* v. *Fulton County Dept. of Family & Childrens' Services*, 563 F.2d 1200 (1977), *cert. denied*, 98 S. Ct. 3103 (1978), where the agency, without a hearing, removed a 2-year-old child of mixed race from his "excellent" white foster parents (who wished to adopt him) in order to place the child with then-unidentified black parents.

See also news reports of a grandmother "who has cared for her grandson since he was six weeks old . . . [being] told that . . . she is too old to look after him anymore. 'I am heartbroken,' said Mrs. Hannah Taylor . . . as more than 40 neighbours signed a protest petition against Bedfordshire county council's decision to put the boy [Gregory] in a children's home." Guy Rais, 'Too Old' at 57 to Foster Own Grandson (*Daily Telegraph*, p. 3. col. 1, London, Jan. 29, 1947). In response to the authorities' charge that Mrs. Taylor had signed away her rights over Gregory in 1975, she said: "I went to the council for help because I was short of money. To look after him I had to give up my part-time cleaning job and I only had my widow's pension. They said it would be best if they took him into care although he would still be living with me. It meant I could claim £9 a week allowance as a foster parent. They did not tell me this gave them the right to take him away. If I had known I would never have taken their money. I would have struggled through somehow. I only wish now that I had barricaded myself in when they came to take him away." Early in December 1978, when the social workers came for Gregory, they found him "hid in the scullery." A Correspondent, "Why Widow 'Signed Away' Grandchild" (*The Guardian,* Manchester, Jan. 30, 1979).

In *Stanley* v. *Illinois,* 405 U.S. 645, 647 (1971), the Supreme Court held that an unwed father was entitled to a hearing before the state could take custody of his two children after the death of the mother.

> This Court has not, however, embraced the general proposition that a wrong may be done if it can be undone. . . . Surely, in the case before us, if there is a delay between the doing and the undoing [the father] suffers from the deprivation of his children, and the children suffer from uncertainty and dislocation.

On holding agents of the state accountable for such actions, see para. 10.14 defining "Violation of Family Integrity," para. 10.15 defining "Child Abuse by the State," and para. 40.0 on "Immunity from Liability" of *Appendix* II.

17. *Beyond the Best Interests of the Child* (pp. 42–45).

18. The *Appleton* case is an actual case; the names used are fictitious. For a similar case with an even more tragic ending, see the Maria Colwell case in Appendix I.

19. For additional examples of courts failing to distinguish between the cause of action concerning a child and the appropriate remedy, see *Matter of Nehar* v. *Uhlar*, 43 N.Y.2d 242 (1977). In *Nehar* the court took two children from their mother, where they had lived for 4 years, and returned them to the father from whom the mother abducted them after he had received custody in a divorce proceeding. In observing that "[t]his court has recognized that if the best interests of *all* children are to be served, the abduction of children to avoid the effect of custody decrees must be deterred," Chief Judge Breitel declared:

> Applying these principles and considering the best interest of the children the father is entitled to custody because the [divorce] court so decreed, because he is a fit parent, because the mother obtained the possession of the children by lawless self-help, because the transitory harm caused by disruption past and future was caused by the mother, and because there is insufficient showing that the harm to the children if they be returned to the father is any more irreparable than that caused by the mother in creating the situation in the first instance. The courts cannot assure the happiness and stability of these children; that only their parents could have done, and, hopefully, can still do [*id.* at 251–52].

And see *Matter of the Adoption of a Child by I.T. and K.T.*, 162 N.J. Super. 587, 394 A.2d 120, 127 (Cty. Prob. Ct. 1978). In that case, the court removed a 1-year-old child from the custody of his adoptive parents, even though his natural parents were not seeking his return. The adoptive parents had privately negotiated custody of the child from an attorney who was unlicensed to place children for adoption. Since the "black market" in adoption violated New Jersey law, the court voided the placement and made the child a ward of the state.

> All too often when the principle of "best interests of the child" is urged upon a court it is calculated to preserve the *status quo* and intended to end the matter. Such a reflexive response would demand abdication by the court of its mandate to exact compliance with the legislative scheme. The application of the principle calls for an agonizing reconciliation of competing interests and values. [The suggestion to leave the child with his parents is wrong because] in the first place it casts aside the rights outstanding of the biological parents which have not been extinguished by judicial decree. In the second place, it fails to take account of the interests of society in eliminating the free enterprise market in babies [*id.* at 127].

The appellate court reversed the decision in *Matter of the Adoption of a Child by I.T. and K.T.*, 164 N.J. Super. 476, 486, 397 A.2d 341, 345–46 (1978):

> The enforcement of the criminal laws is a matter separate and apart from the function of an adoption proceeding, and the deterrence of possible criminal sanctions must suffice as the sole remedy chosen by the Legislature. . . . The court's function, therefore, in this connection is simply to report the apparent violations to the

prosecutor, as the trial judge did in this case, so that he may determine whether to invoke the criminal process. It does not extend to the function of applying the criminal laws relating to placement so as to prevent an otherwise valid adoption.

CHAPTER 5:   GROSS FAILURES OF PARENTAL CARE

1. See *Beyond the Best Interests of the Child* (pp. 33–36, 47–49, 145–46).

2. *Comerford* v. *Cherry*, 100 So.2d 385, 390 (Fla. 1958). The court also said:

    The courts have always seen to it that the property of a testator was received by those whom the testator indicated. The upbringing of minor children is a matter which concerns every thoughtful human being more vitally than the disposition of his worldly possessions when he has passed on.

3. *Welfare Commissioner* v. *Anonymous*, 33 Conn. Sup. 100, 364 A.2d 250 (1976).

4. *Id.* at 101–02, 364 A.2d at 251–52.

5. Indeed Judge Rubinow recognized the undesirability of the Commissioner initiating an adjudication. He observed that "the court would not adopt [the commissioner's construction] for a reason of 'policy.' That 'policy' reason is that, in construing a statute concerning the relationship of children to biological or nonbio-

logical parents, courts should prefer that construction which minimizes state intervention" [*id.* at 102, A.2d at 252].

And see *Matter of D*, 547, P.2d 175, 182 (1976) construing the following statutory exception in ORS 109.322 to the general rule that the consent of parents is a prerequisite to issuance of an adoption order:

> "If either parent . . . is imprisoned in a state or federal prison under a sentence for a term of not less than three years, there shall be served upon such parent, if he has not consented in writing to the adoption, a citation in accordance with ORS 109.330 to show cause why the adoption of the child should not be decreed. . . . Upon hearing being had, if the court finds that the welfare of the child will be best promoted through the adoption of the child, the consent of the . . . imprisoned parent is not required, and the court shall have authority to proceed regardless of the objection of such parent. . . ."

6. See S. Freud, Three Essays on the Theory of Sexuality [1905]. In *Standard Edition*, 7:173–79, 222–31 (London: Hogarth Press, 1953); Lauretta Bender and Abraham Blau, The Reaction of Children to Sexual Relations with Adults (*Amer. J. Orthopsychiat.*, 7:500–18, 1937); Louis J. Doshay, *The Boy Sex Offender and His Later Career* (New York: Grune & Stratton, 1943); B. Cormier, M. Kennedy, and S. Kennedy, Psychodynamics of Father-Daughter Incest (*Canad. Psychiat. Assn. J.*, 7:203, 1962); D. Swanson, Adult Sexual Abuse of Children (*Dis. Nerv. Syst.*, 29:677–83, 1968); T. Shonfelder, Sexual Trauma in Childhood and Its Consequences (*Praxis Psychother.*, 15:12–20, 1970); S. L.

Kaplan and E. Poznanski, Child Psychiatric Patients Who Share a Bed with a Parent (*J. Amer. Acad. Child Psychiat.*, 13:344–56, 1974); Ruth S. and C. Henry Kempe, *Child Abuse* (Cambridge, Mass.: Harvard University Press, Developing Child Series, 1978).

7. See S. Freud, Katharina [1893–95]. In *Standard Edition*, 2:125–34 (London: Hogarth Press, 1955); A. Rasmussen, The Importance of Sexual Attacks on Children Less than 14 Years of Age for the Development of Mental Diseases and Character Anomalies (*Acta Psychiat. Neurol.*, 9:351, 1934); August Aichhorn, On the Technique of Child Guidance [1936]. In *Delinquency and Child Guidance*, ed. O. Fleischmann, P. Kramer, and H. Ross (New York: International Universities Press, 1964, pp. 101–92); P. Sloane and E. Karpinski, Effects of Incest upon the Participants (*Amer. J. Orthopsychiat.*, 12:666, 1952); I. Kaufman, A. Peck, and L. Tagiori, The Family Constellation and Overt Incestuous Relations between Father and Daughter (*ibid.*, 24:266–79, 1954); A. Yozukoglu and J. P. Kemph, Children Not Severely Damaged by Incest with a Parent (*J. Amer. Acad. Child Psychiat.*, 5:111–24, 1966); M. S. Adams and J. B. Neel, Children of Incest (*Pediatrics*, 40:55, 1967); Melvin Lewis and P. M. Sarrel, Some Psychological Aspects of Seduction, Incest, and Rape in Childhood (*J. Amer. Acad. Child Psychiat.*, 8:606–19, 1969); Incest and Family Disorder: Editorial (*Brit. Med. J.*, 5810:364–65, 1972); N. Lukianowicz, Incest (*Brit. J. Psychiat.*, 120:301–13, 1972); A. Katan, Children Who Were Raped. In *The Psychoanalytic Study of the Child*, 28:208–24 (New Haven: Yale University Press, 1973); M. Margolis, A Preliminary Report of a Case of Consummated Mother-

Son Incest. In *Annual of Psychoanalysis*, 5:267–94 (New York: International Universities Press, 1977); A. Rosenfeld, C. Nadelson, M. Krieger, and J. Backman, Incest and Sexual Abuse of Children (*J. Amer. Acad. Child Psychiat.*, 16:334–46, 1977); K. N. Dixon et al., Father-Son Incest (*Amer. J. Psychiat.*, 135:835–38, 1978).

8. See S. Freud, The Interpretation of Dreams [1900]. In *Standard Edition*, 5:398–99 (London: Hogarth Press, 1953); *idem*, Dissolution of the Oedipus Complex [1924] (*ibid.*, 19:176–79, 1961); *idem*, Some Psychological Consequences of the Anatomical Distinction between the Sexes [1925] (*ibid.*, 19:243–61, 1961); M. Gitelson, Re-Evaluation of the Rôle of the Oedipus Complex (*Int. J. Psycho-Anal.*, 33:351–54, 1952); J. Lampl-de Groot, Re-Evaluation of the Rôle of the Oedipus Complex (*ibid.*, 33:335–42, 1952); Lilli Peller, Libidinal Phases, Ego Development and Play. In *The Psychoanalytic Study of the Child*, 9:178–98 (New York: International Universities Press, 1954); A. Freud, *Normality and Pathology in Childhood*. In *The Writings of Anna Freud*, Vol. 6 (*supra*); Humberto Nagera, ed., *Basic Psychoanalytic Concepts on the Libido Theory* (New York: Basic Books, The Hampstead Clinic Psychoanalytic Library, 1969, 1:64–82).

9. Ray E. Helfer and C. Henry Kempe, *Child Abuse and Neglect* (Cambridge, Mass.: Ballinger Publishing Co., 1976, p. 148):

> It is evident that typical community intervention in incest cases, rather than being constructive, has the effect of a knockout blow to a family already weakened by serious internal stresses.

10. See, e.g., *In re Armentrout*, 207 Kan. 366, 485 P.2d 183 (1971) (termination of parental rights to child after stepfather was convicted of statutory rape of minor daughter). An acquittal by reason of insanity rests on the presumption or an actual finding that the accused is "guilty" of the crime charged beyond a reasonable doubt. See generally J. Goldstein and J. Katz, "Abolish the Insanity Defense—Why Not?" 72 *Yale L. J.*, 853 (1963) and J. Goldstein, "The *Brawner* Rule—Why? Or No More Nonsense on Non Sense in the Criminal Law Please!" 1973 *Wash. U. L. Quart.*, 126 (1973).

11. Institute of Judicial Administration/American Bar Association Joint Commission on Juvenile Justice Standards, *Standards Relating to Abuse and Neglect: Tentative Draft* (Cambridge, Mass.: Ballinger Publishing Co., 1977, §2.1D, at p. 58).

12. *Id.* at 60.

13. *Id.*

14. *In re Vulon Children*, 288 N.Y.S.2d 203, 56 Misc.2d 19 (1968).

15. *Id.* at 206–09, 56 Misc.2d at 21–24. Judge Dembitz noted:

> No formal opinion was rendered at the time of dismissal, though the reasons therefor were indicated. In view of a notice of appeal by the Bureau of Child Welfare and the often expressed appellate view that a statement of the trial court's reasons is important for adequate review, this opinion setting forth more fully the grounds

for dismissing the petition is now rendered [*id.* at 205, n. 1, 56 Misc.2d at 205, n.].

16. Under §483-d of the New York Penal Law (McKinney's 1967), doctors and surgeons treating a child have a duty to report to an appropriate public welfare official any case where there is "reason to believe that such child has had serious injury or injuries inflicted upon him or her as a result of abuse or neglect. . . ." As to the social desirability of such reporting laws, see Paulsen, Child Abuse Reporting Laws, 67 *Colum. L. Rev.*, 1 (1967). See p. 48 note † and pp. 228–30 note 13.

17. See Hugh Bevan, Should Reporting Be Mandatory? In *Concerning Child Abuse,* ed. A. W. Franklin (Edinburgh, London, and New York: Churchill Livingston, 1975, p. 134):

No decision was reached on the question of mandatory reporting. On the one hand some felt that this would improve the prospects of proper communication between the professionals involved in a case. Others believed that notification by itself unsupported by action accomplished nothing. It might indeed place obstacles in the way of good management. Medical freedom of action would be impeded. Families might be even more afraid of the consequences of seeking help or might panic and leave the area. The essentials were the case conference at which information would be exchanged and the growth of trust between the individual workers and the agencies which they represented. There were difficult problems of who should report what to whom.

But see Ruth S. and C. Henry Kempe, *Child Abuse* (*supra*, p. 8):

> As public attitudes become more broadly under-standing, many more parents voluntarily seek help before they seriously harm their children. In 1968, California had 4,000 reported cases; in 1972, 40,000; Florida's reports jumped from 10 cases to 30,000 over the same four years, and Michigan's went from 721 to 30,000. Not only are more cases being reported—they are of a milder nature, suggesting that families are being helped sooner. In Denver, the number of hos-pitalized abused children who die from their injuries has dropped from 20 a year (between 1960 and 1975) to less than one a year.

18. See, e.g., James Collie, The Police Role. In *Concerning Child Abuse*, ed. A. W. Franklin (*supra*, p. 124):

> The NSPC in its study entitled *78 Battered Children* (1969) commented 'The unsatisfactory aftercare arrangements made by many hospitals despite the evidence of repeated unexplained injury is disturbing. Two out of every five chil-dren admitted because of injury had previously been injured to an extent sufficient to warrant medical attention. Three out of every five who were discharged home after medical treatment had to be re-admitted on account of subsequent injury', and 'The efficacy of investigation proce-dures frequently described in the records is ques-tionable.' (Page 20.)

19. See Alfred White Franklin, ed., *Concerning Child Abuse* (*supra*); see especially Hugh Bevan, Should Reporting

Be Mandatory? (pp. 133–35); James Collie, The Police
Role (pp. 123–26); Selwyn Smith, Ruth Hanson, and
Sheila Noble, Parents of Battered Children (pp. 41–
48). See also Ray E. Helfer and C. Henry Kempe,
Child Abuse and Neglect (*supra*); Department of Chil-
dren and Youth Services, State of Connecticut, *Child
Abuse and Neglect: The Connecticut Mandated Re-
porter's Handbook* (June 1978); Sanford N. Katz,
Melba McGrath, Ruth-Arlene Howe, *Child Neglect
Laws in America* (*supra*).

20.   See notes 17 and 19 (this chapter) and Appendix I.

21.   Selwyn M. Smith, Ruth Hanson, and Sheila Noble,
Parents of Battered Children (*supra*, p. 48):

> Oliver and Cox (1973) showed that the
> tendency to perpetuate child abuse in successive
> generations is not diminished by supplying ex-
> tensive medical and social help to battering
> parents. Furthermore, 60 per cent of children
> who are returned home are rebattered (Skinner
> and Castle, 1969). While every effort must be
> made to rehabilitate battering parents this
> should not be at the expense of the safety of the
> child. In the light of our findings we believe that
> strong consideration should be given to perma-
> nent removal of children from parental care in
> those cases where after an overall psychiatric
> assessment the likelihood of parents responding
> to treatment is thought to be remote.

22.   It is, however, a matter for legislation that the state
prohibit teachers, at least in a compulsory education
system, from using corporal punishment as a mode of

discipline. Though the authority to use such punishment may not violate some constitutions, there is no justification for its continued legalization. In *Ingraham* v. *Wright*, 430 U.S. 651, 664, 97 S.Ct. 1401, 1405 (1977), the United States Supreme Court upheld the constitutionality of corporal punishment in the public schools. In that case, two junior high school students had been struck on the buttocks with the authorized "flat wooden paddle measuring less than two feet long, three to four inches wide, and about one-half inch thick." Because one of the students "was slow to respond to his teacher's instructions" he "was subjected to more than 20 licks with a paddle while being held over a table in the principal's office. The paddling was so severe that he suffered a hematoma requiring medical attention and keeping him out of school for several days. Andrews [the other student] was paddled several times for minor infractions. On two occasions he was struck on his arms, once depriving him of the full use of his arm for a week."

But see John Vinocur, Swedes Shun Norse Adage, Ban Spanking (New York *Times,* April 4, 1979, p. A7, cols. 1–6):

> As hard as six members of the Swedish Parliament pressed the arguments for the rod— from the Eddas, 13th-century Nordic mythological works in poetry and prose; from early Swedish statutes, and from the Old Testament— 259 of their colleagues have voted for a law saying that, starting July 1, parents may not strike their children or treat them in any other humiliating way. . . . Spanking is out, and although the matter of humiliating treatment is vague, a refusal to talk to children, depriving

them of a meal or peeking into their mail seems to be illegal too.

"It is a totally absurd, totally ridiculous law, the kind of thing that means nothing and cannot be interpreted or enforced," said Allan Akerlind, one of those who voted against it. The father of five, he plans to go on administering his own form [of] family justice. . . .

While Mr. Akerlind evoked visions of children lining up at police stations to complain about their parents, Mr. Ekdahl and a Ministry of Justice spokesman, Sten Lindberg, said they viewed this as extremely unlikely. "We have tried to make it clear that this is a pedagogic law," Mr. Lindberg said. We hope to use the law to change attitudes. If we launched a big campaign on the subject, it probably would be forgotten in a year. But the law stays, and it enters the public consciousness."

23. For the wording of such statutes see the neglect laws that are collected in S. Katz, M. McGrath, and R.-A. Howe, *Child Neglect Laws in America* (*supra*). See also note 25 (this chapter).

See also R. K. Uviller, Child-Abuse in Snooping (New York *Times*, April 20, 1977, op. ed. p., col. 3):

"Emotional neglect" is meaningless because it is so subjective and virtually impossible to disprove. It serves no purpose—unless, of course, it is designed to provide social welfare bureaucrats with bigger and better empires.

24. Institute of Judicial Administration/American Bar Association Joint Commission on Juvenile Justice Standards, *Standards Relating to Abuse and Neglect* (*supra*,

§2.1C, at pp. 55–56). See also Wald, State Intervention on Behalf of 'Neglected' Children: A Search for Realistic Standards, 27 *Stan. L. Rev.*, 985, 1019 (1975).

25. American Bar Association Joint Commission on Juvenile Justice Standards, *Standards Relating to Abuse and Neglect* (*supra*, at pp. 55–56):

> C. [Coercive intervention should be authorized when] a child is suffering serious emotional damage, evidenced by severe anxiety, depression, or withdrawal, or untoward aggressive behavior toward self or others, and the child's parents are not willing to provide treatment for him/her.
>
> *Commentary*
> . . . The definition should place sufficient constraints on expert testimony and judicial decisionmaking so that it will not be based solely on individual views regarding proper child development. It is possible that in practice this definition will prove either too broad or too narrow. These standards should not be considered frozen. Periodic review to see how they are working and to incorporate new knowledge is essential.
>
> The standard limits intervention to situations where the child is actually evidencing the symptoms. Intervention may not be premised on the prediction of harm. . . .
>
> The standard does not require that emotional damage be caused by parental conduct. If a child evidences serious damage and the parent is unwilling to provide help, intervention is justified regardless of the cause of the harm [*id.* at 57–58].

26. This is based on an actual case.

27. *Roe et al.* v. *Conn,* 417 F. Supp. 769, 775 (M.D. Ala. 1976).

28. Deposition of patrolman L. T. Conn, Sept. 1975 (pp. 250–56) in *Roe et al.* v. *Conn,* Civ. No. 75–232-N (M.D. Ala. 1976).

29. *Roe et al.* v. *Conn,* 417 F. Supp. 769, 774–75 (M.D. Ala. 1976). Judge Rives held that the Alabama Code provision "which authorizes summary seizure of a child 'if it appears that . . . the child is in such condition that its welfare requires,' violates procedural due process under the Fourteenth Amendment of the United States Constitution." He said:

> The facts of this case dispel any notion that the State was faced with an emergency situation. As we earlier found, Officer Conn's investigation revealed that Richard Roe was clothed, clean and in "fairly good" physical condition with no signs of physical abuse. The Wambles' home was "relatively clean" and stocked with "adequate food." Without danger of immediate harm or threatened harm to the child, the State's interest in protecting the child is not sufficient to justify a removal of the child prior to notice and a hearing. Additionally, even in the event summary seizure had been justified, a hearing would have had to follow the seizure "as soon as practicable" and not six weeks later as it did in the present case . . . [*id.* at 778].

30. *Alsager* v. *District Court of Polk County, Iowa,* 406 F. Supp. 10 (S.D. Iowa 1975).

31. Daniel St. Albin Greene, They Lost Their Kids for Six Years (*The National Observer*, p. 1, p. 14, Col. 2, May 29, 1976).

32. *Alsager* v. *District Court of Polk County, Iowa*, 406 F. Supp. 10, 13 (S.D. Iowa 1975).

33. *Id.* at 22.

34. *Id.* at 23. The U.S. Court of Appeals affirmed the U.S. District Court's holding that the termination of parental rights proceedings were unconstitutional. However, it limited its finding of unconstitutionality to the procedures which were followed and did not address the question of whether the Iowa statute was unconstitutionally vague. The District Court had held that the statute was void for vagueness. *Alsager* v. *District Court of Polk County, Iowa*, 545 F.2d 1137 (8th Cir. 1976).

35. See para. 10.14, para. 10.15, and para. 40.0, Appendix II, *infra*.

36. This is based on an actual case.

37. This is based on an actual case.

38. This is based on an actual case.

CHAPTER 6: REFUSAL BY PARENTS TO AUTHORIZE LIFESAVING MEDICAL CARE

1. See J. Goldstein, Psychoanalysis and Jurisprudence, 77 *Yale L. J.* 1053, 1059 (1968); and see note 13 (Chapter 4).

2. These standards are anchored in such common-law notions as that of plain duty. See Justice Field's jury charge regarding criminal liability for acts of omission in *United States* v. *Knowles*, 26 F. Cas. 800, 801 (N.D. Cal. 1864) (No. 15, 540):

> [T]he duty omitted must be a plain duty, by which I mean that it must be one that does not admit of any discussion as to its obligatory force; one upon which different minds must agree, or will generally agree. Where doubt exists as to what conduct should be pursued in a particular case, and intelligent men differ as to the proper action to be had, the law does not impute guilt to any one if, from omission to adopt one course instead of another, fatal consequences follow to others.

3. *In the Matter of Joseph Hofbauer*, Saratoga County Family Court, June 28, 1978, *aff'd*, New York Supreme Court, November 22, 1978 (slip opinion) presents an example in which the criteria for intervention under this ground were not met.

Eight-year-old Joseph was diagnosed as having Hodgkin's disease. After refusing medical treatment consisting of radiation and possibly chemotherapy, Joseph's parents placed him in a course of nutritional or metabolic therapy that included the use of laetrile. The State of New York, through its Commissioner of Health and of Social Services, charged that by doing so, the Hofbauers had neglected Joseph, and sought to remove Joseph from his home. During the neglect hearing, doctors for the state testified that radiation with or without chemotherapy was the conventional treatment for Joseph's disease, that such treatment presented serious risks, and that no scientific foundation for metabolic therapy existed. Doctors testifying for the Hofbauers asserted that positive evidence for such therapy exists.

Family Court Judge Loren N. Brown, in a thoughtful opinion, found that the Hofbauers are "loving parents who have devoted more time and energy and have given more thought and concern to the care of their child than would be expected of the ordinary parent," and that the requirement of providing adequate medical care only requires that parents place their child under the care of a licensed physician. Of several treatment alternatives, the Hofbauers had simply chosen that "least acceptable to the conventional medical establishment." Under these circumstances therefore, where concerned parents chose for their child medically supported though unconventional treatment, the court refused to override that choice and find Joseph a neglected child.

On appeal, New York State Supreme Court Judge Michael Sweeney noted that the critical issue was whether Joseph's parents had supplied him with adequate medical care. Unlike the trial court, however, he held that due to the seriousness of Joseph's disease, adequate medical care might entail more than placing the child under the care of a licensed physician. Nonetheless, he found significant the concern shown by Joseph's parents, the evidence that nutritional therapy was currently controlling Joseph's condition, and the fact that both Joseph's parents and the doctor they had chosen for Joseph would agree to conventional therapy if his condition so warranted. Judge Sweeney therefore affirmed the trial court's decision. In reaching that conclusion, he relied upon what was for him a firmly established principle of law:

> The primary right, duty and privilege to select the type of medical care to be given and the physician to administer it belongs to the parent.

4. *In re Pogue,* No. M-18–74 (D.C. Sup. Ct. Nov. 11, 1974), reported in *The Washington Post,* Thursday, November 14, 1974, §C, p. 1, col. 1.

5. Kelsey, Shall These Children Live? A Conversation with Dr. Raymond S. Duff (*Reflection,* 72:4, 7, 1975). For other expressions of Dr. Duff's views, see R. S. Duff and A. Y. M. Campbell, Moral and Ethical Dilemmas in the Special-Care Nursery (*New England J. Med.,* 289:885, 1973); *idem,* On Deciding the Care of Severely Handicapped or Dying Persons: With Particular Reference to Infants (*Pediatrics,* 57:487, 1976).

6. See generally S. Provence and R. C. Lipton, *Infants in Institutions* (New York: International Universities Press, 1962, pp. 159–66).

   For a description of the conditions in one institution, New York's Willowbrook State School for the Mentally Retarded, see Judge Judd's opinion in *New York State Ass'n for Retarded Children, Inc.* v. *Rockefeller,* 357 F. Supp. 752, 755–57 (E.D.N.Y. 1973). Referring to the "inhumane" conditions at the school, Judge Judd mentioned the "loss of an eye, the breaking of teeth, the loss of part of an ear bitten off by another resident, and frequent bruises and scalp wounds" as typical complaints.

   For an effort to reverse the course of the past, see *Consent Judgment in the Willowbrook Case,* No. 72 Civ. 356/357 (E.D.N.Y. Apr. 30, 1975). Similarly, see *Wyatt* v. *Stickney,* 344 F. Supp. 387 (M.D. Ala. 1972), which has been described as "dealing with a remote, rural state institution in Alabama housing some five thousand retarded children in conditions of unrelieved horror." Burt, Developing Constitutional Rights Of, In, and For Children (*Law and Contemporary Problems*, 39:118, 138, 1975). And see Statement of D. S. Days, III, Assistant Attorney General, Civil Rights Division, before the Committee on Human Resources, Subcommittee on Child and Human Development, U.S. Senate, Concerning the Abuse of Children (Jan. 24, 1979).

7. From a conversation with Judge James H. Lincoln, Judge of the Probate Court, Juvenile Division, Wayne County, Michigan.

8. J. E. Schowalter, J. B. Ferholt, and N. M. Mann, The Adolescent Patient's Decision to Die (*Pediatrics*, 51: 97–98, 1973).

9. See, e.g., S. 8, Family Law Reform Act (1969), which provides that any person aged 16 may give consent to any surgical, medical, or dental treatment to himself; and note 12 (Chapter 7).

For a discussion of emancipation of children for health care purposes, see J. Goldstein, Medical Care for the Child at Risk: On State Supervention of Parental Autonomy, 86 *Yale L. J.* 645, 661–64 (1977). Also see, e.g., *In Re Roger S.*, 19 C.3d 921, 929, 141 Cal. Rptr. 298, 302, 569 P.2d 1286, 1290 (1977), in which the court acknowledged that since it is within a parent's power to place the child in a state-operated mental hospital and require him to remain there, just as he may place the child in a public hospital for treatment of a physical condition, it follows that he may waive those due process rights that the child might assert if the state sought hospitalization. But the court held that "as to minors 14 years of age or older, the parental power is not this comprehensive. The consequences of confining a person, minor or adult, involuntarily in a mental institution . . . impinge much more directly on the liberty interest of the patient than does confinement for treatment of physical illness." On emancipation for the purpose of obtaining legal assistance, see Chapter 7, pp. 126–29.

For an interesting illustration of a parental decision to respect the wishes of their 10-year-old child not to continue treatment, see *The Denver Post*, Sunday, December 4, 1978, p. 38, col. 3:

> Shawn, who died of a rare form of cancer . . . had discussed his decision in a tape-recorded session with the Rev. Richard Olson of the First Baptist Church in Racine.

> "Mom and Dad came in, and the doctors came in . . . they said it probably wouldn't work, and if it did work, it would stop working sooner or later and I would die. Or I could just go off treatment, you know, and just, you know, stay at home and just die.

> *   *   *

> "When I found out I had cancer, I just thought, 'God'll take care of that,' . . . And he did. Not the way I wanted him to. . . . He always answers a prayer, but not always the way you want him to answer it."

> Shawn died of Rhabdomyosarcoma, a fast-spreading cancer that attacks the soft-muscle

tissue. Radiation and chemotherapy treatments helped only temporarily, his mother said. By the time the disease was discovered, it already had invaded his lungs.

About a month ago, doctors suggested a more extreme, physically taxing drug treatment that would offer no hope for a cure but might prolong his life.

"At the most it would give him some more time," [they said]. But the Bonenbergers asked that Shawn make his own decision, and he decided to live a day at a time.

"You just have as much fun as you can and make use of it," Shawn told Olson. "It's like each day is a gift. Like if you say, 'I'm going to clean my room tomorrow,' tomorrow you might not be here. You never know. You just live one day at a time.

* * *

"I've never really accepted the fact that I have cancer. It's just hard. . . . A lot of people, when they find out they have cancer, they just give up. I definitely didn't do that."

10. *In re Sampson*, 65 Misc. 2d 658, 317 N.Y.S.2d 641 (Fam. Ct. 1970) *aff'd*, 37 App. Div. 2d 668, 323 N.Y.S. 2d 253 (1971), *aff'd*, 29 N.Y.2d 900, 278 N.E.2d 918, 328 N.Y.S.2d 686 (1972).

11. *Id.* at 660, 317 N.Y.S.2d at 644.

12. *Id.*, 317 N.Y.S.2d at 644. According to Judge Elwyn, a

psychologist had found Kevin to be extremely dependent. The staff psychiatrist reported that Kevin dem-
onstrated " 'inferiority feeling and low self concept.' "
Id., 317 N.Y.S.2d at 644.

13. *Id.* at 672, 317 N.Y.S.2d at 655.

14. *Id.* at 673, 317 N.Y.S.2d at 656 (quoting *In re Seiferth*,
309 N.Y. 80, 87, 127 N.E.2d 820, 824 (1955) (J. Fuld,
dissenting). For a contrary view of the importance of
a child's preference regarding surgery, see *In re Green*,
448 Pa. 338, 292, A.2d 387 (1972). Ricky Green was
then 15 years old and had a 94° curvature of the spine
as the result of polio. Doctors proposed a spinal fusion
to straighten the spine, but Ricky's mother refused her
consent for blood transfusions during the operation.
Saying that the "ultimate question" concerned Ricky's
wishes, the Pennsylvania Supreme Court remanded the
case for a determination of Ricky's wishes. *Id.* at 350,
292 A.2d at 392. After talking with Ricky, the trial
judge found that he did not want the operation; his
wishes were honored. *Green Appeal*, 452 Pa. 373, 307
A.2d 279 (1973).

15. 65 Misc. 2d at 674, 317 N.Y.S.2d at 657.

16. *In re Seiferth*, 309 N.Y. 80, 127 N.E.2d 820 (1955).

17. Letter from William G. Conable, attorney for Seiferth,
to Joseph Goldstein (Apr. 20, 1964), quoted in J. Goldstein & Jay Katz, *The Family and the Law* (New
York: Free Press, 1965, p. 993).

18. Letter from Mr. Elmer R. Weil, county attorney of

Erie County, to Joseph Goldstein (Apr. 28, 1964), quoted in *id.* at 993–94.

19. *Hart* v. *Brown*, 29 Conn. Supp. 368, 289 A.2d 386 (1972). See Chapter 2, p. 22, footnote.

20. The doctors were willing to rely on parental consent, without court review, to remove both of Katheleen's kidneys and thus leave her with "no potential kidney function" and with the "prospect of survival . . . because of her age, at best questionable." *Id.* at 372, 289 A.2d at 388. Compare *In re Nemser*, 51 Misc. 2d 616. 621–25, 273 N.Y.S.2d 624, 629–32 (1966), where the judge criticized the modern tendency for doctors to seek judicial approval for planned operations, even in emergency situations, rather than proceed without the written permission of the patient's guardian.

21. It may be that parental consent to surgery for the irreversible sterilization of a child ought not to be sufficient to authorize the operation without court review. In *A.L.* v. *G.R.H.*, 325 N.E.2d 501 (Ind. App. 1975), the court held that a parent does not have a common-law right to have a minor child sterilized. But see *Stump* v. *Sparkman*, 98 S. Ct. 1099 (1978), holding that the mother who requested the sterilization of her daughter without the daughter's knowledge and the judge who ordered it were immune from suit by the daughter for damages.

22. 29 Conn. Supp. at 378, 289 A.2d at 391 (emphasis supplied). For another view of the issues presented by this case, see M. Lewis, Kidney Donation by a 7-Year-Old Identical Twin Child: Psychological, Legal, and Ethical

Considerations (*J. Amer. Acad. Child Psychiat.*, 13:
221–43, 1974). But see *In re Richardson*, 284 So. 2d 185
(La. App.), *cert. denied*, 284 So. 2d 338 (La. 1973),
affirming the lower court's refusal to approve a transplant from a mentally retarded 17-year-old to his 32-
year-old sister; *Howard* v. *Fulton-DeKalb Hosp. Auth.*,
Civ. No. 3–90430 (Sup. Ct., Fulton County, Ga., Nov.
29, 1973), finding invalid a mother's consent to a transplant from her 15-year-old, moderately retarded
daughter, since the mother would be the recipient of
the kidney. The court in *Howard*, however, authorized
the transplant under a doctrine of "substituted judgment." The case, along with others that pose similar
issues, is discussed in Nolan, Anatomical Transplants
Between Family Members: The Problems Facing Court
and Counsel, [1975] *Fam. L. Rep.* (BNA) 4035.

CHAPTER 7: THE CHILD'S NEED FOR LEGAL ASSISTANCE

1. *Beyond the Best Interests of the Child* (p. 100, para.
30.4). Also see Institute of Judicial Administration/
American Bar Association Joint Commission on Juvenile Justice Standards, *Standards Relating to Abuse
and Neglect* (*supra*, 5.1E at p. 96):

> E. Appointment of counsel for child. Upon
> filing, the court should be required to ap-
> point counsel at public expense to represent
> the child identified in the petition, as a
> party to the proceedings. . . .

> *Commentary*

> This subsection mandates the appointment
> of counsel for the child named in the peti-
> tion. There are good reasons to believe this

> guarantee is constitutionally mandated in light of the significant consequences to the child if court wardship were ultimately imposed. . . . The reasoning underlying the Supreme Court's mandate of counsel for minors in *In re Gault*, 387 U.S. 1 (1967) thus applies readily to minors involved in wardship proceedings (though *Gault* itself applied only to proceedings in which the child was charged with conduct that would be criminal if performed by an adult). . . .

But see this Chapter, pp. 126–29.

2. In *Ingraham* v. *Wright*, 430 U.S. 651, 670, (1977), Mr. Justice Powell alludes to the insulating function parents may serve:

> The schoolchild has little need for the protection of the Eighth Amendment. . . . Even while at school, the child brings with him the support of family and friends and is rarely apart from teachers and other pupils who may witness and protest any instances of mistreatment.

3. Children who are adjudicated to be the responsibility of their longtime caretakers, under the ground described in Chapter 4, would not require counsel because disposition would generally be automatic. Except for the special category of older children for whom the question of custody requires a hearing, not to appoint counsel would accord with the least intrusive disposition principle.

   Lawyers for children may unnecessarily contribute to the litigiousness of placement proceedings. See Strauss and Strauss, Book Review, 74 *Colum. L.*

Rev. 996 (1974), and Dembitz, Book Review, 83 *Yale L. J.*, 1304 (1974).

4. See Rule 23 of the Federal Rules of Civil Procedure (class actions), and discussion in Wright, 7 *Federal Practice and Procedure* §§1751–1753 (1972).

5. See Amici Brief for A Group of Concerned Persons for Children at 12–13, *Smith* v. *Organization of Foster Families,* 431 U.S. 816 (1977):

> Just as appointment of counsel for children in a divorce custody dispute or neglect proceeding does not foreclose the right of separating or allegedly neglecting parents to speak for their children, so the appointment of Helen L. Buttenwieser [by the court to represent foster children as a class] does not vitiate the standing of the long term foster parents in this case to speak for the children entrusted to their care. A scrupulous concern for possible conflict of interest led to the appointment of *separate* but *not* of *exclusive* representation for the children.
>
> Separate counsel for the foster children [as a class, not as individuals] was appointed because the District Court believed that counsel for the foster parents could not "provide effective assistance to the court in defining, articulating and exploring those interests of the children which are *potentially* adverse to those of the foster parents." Her function was to serve as a fail-safe mechanism — to insure that all points of view were presented. But her voice was not intended to silence all others. None of her clients, not even the originally named foster chil-

dren, could instruct her as to their desires, ignore her advice, express dissatisfaction with her representation or engage other counsel. She could not be and was never intended to be the final arbiter of the interests of even one child — much less a whole class of children.

Rule 23(c) of the Federal Rules of Civil Procedure, to assure fairness, requires that notice in some class actions be given to all members of the class, the exclusion of persons who so request from the class, and the allowance of appearance through counsel by any member of the class.

6. See *Beyond the Best Interests of the Child* (p. 100, para. 30.4).

7. This is based on an actual case.

8. Counsel must avoid becoming rubber stamps for court or agency. See, e.g., *Wisconsin ex rel. Memmel* v. *Mundy*, 75 Wis. 2d 276, 277, 249 N.W.2d 573, 574 (1977), where the parties stipulated that "all persons involuntarily committed to the [Milwaukee County mental health] center . . . had been denied their constitutional rights to effective assistance of counsel and due process of law." In *de Montigny* v. *de Montigny*, 70 Wis. 2d 131, 141, 233 N.W.2d 463, 468–69 (1975), the court held:

> The guardian *ad litem* is more than an adjunct to the court. He is the attorney for the children and their interests. He must perform his duties in accordance with the standards of professional responsibility adopted by this court. Code of Professional Responsibility, 43 Wis. 2d, Decem-

ber 16, 1969. Nominal representation that fails to assure that children are treated as parties to the action is insufficient and constitutes a breach of the duties of professional responsibility.

The Code of Professional Responsibility, Canon 7, EC 7–12, states:

If the disability of a client and the lack of a legal representative compel the lawyer to make decisions for his client, the lawyer should consider all circumstances then prevailing and act with care to safeguard and advance the interests of his client.

9. *G.* v. *G.*, Conn. Super. Ct. No. 11 28 46 (April 6, 1977) (unreported opinion).

10. See *Beyond the Best Interests of the Child* (p. 38).

11. See J. Goldstein, On Being Adult and Being An Adult in Secular Law (*Daedalus,* 105:69, 71, 1976).

12. For an interesting proposal on the emancipation of minors, see California Senate Bill 1473 to amend Division 1 of the Civil Code, effective January, 1979, reported in 305 F.L.R. 0013–14 (1978).

LEGISLATIVE COUNSEL'S DIGEST
SB 1473, Behr. Minors.

At common law a minor may be emancipated by an act of his parent, or by his marriage, or by his enlistment in the military service.

This bill would require the court to sustain the petition if it finds that the minor is a person described by its provisions and no parent or guardian appears at the hearing and objects, and would require the court to deny the petition if it finds that emancipation would not be in the minor's best interest. . . .

PART 2.7   EMANCIPATION OF MINORS

61. The Legislature finds and declares that the case law of this state is unclear as to the definition and consequences of emancipation of minors; that a legislative statement is required; and that a process should be provided so that emancipated minors can obtain an official declaration of their status. It is the purpose of this part to provide a clear statement defining emancipation and its consequences and to permit an emancipated minor to obtain a court declaration of his status. This part is not intended to affect the status of minors who are now or may become emancipated under present decisional case law.

62. Any person under the age of 18 years who comes within the following description is an emancipated minor:

(a) Who has entered into a valid marriage, whether or not such marriage was terminated by dissolution; or

(b) Who is on active duty with any of the armed forces of the United States of America; or

(c) Who willingly lives separate and apart from his parents or legal guardian, with the consent or acquiescence of the parents or guardian, and who is managing his own financial affairs, regardless of the source of his income so long as it is not derived from any activity declared to be a crime by the laws of the State of California, or declared to be a crime by the laws of the United States.

63.   An emancipated minor shall be considered as being over the age of majority for the following purposes:

(a) For the purpose of consenting to medical, dental, or psychiatric care, without parental consent, knowledge, or liability.

(b) For the purpose of his capacity to enter into a binding contract.

(c) For the purpose of his capacity to sue and be sued in his own name.

(d) For the purpose of his right to support by his parents.

(e) For purposes of the rights of his parents to his earnings, and to control him.

(f) For the purpose of establishing his own residence.

(g) For the purpose of buying or selling real property.

(h) For the purposes of the application of Section 300 and 601 of the Welfare and Institutions Code.

(i) for purposes of applying for a work permit pursuant to Section 49110 of the Education Code without the request of parents or guardians.

(j) For purpose of ending all vicarious liability of the minor's parents or guardian for the minor's torts; provided, that nothing in this section shall affect any liability of a parent, guardian, spouse, or employer imposed by the Vehicle Code, or any vicarious liability which arises from an agency relationship.

(k) For the purpose of enrolling in any school or college.

13. Many state statutes require consideration of a child's wishes in custody proceedings. See generally R. H. Mnookin, *Child, Family and State* (Boston: Little, Brown, 1978, pp. 638–41).

    For an example of an opinion that directly clashes with ours, see the reported comments of a Michigan attorney in 4 F.L.R. 1203, 2842 (1978):

    > The speaker pointed out several areas in which legal aid lawyers should lay plans for precedent-changing litigation, and urged the directions in which it should go—one of these being establishment of the absolute right of the child to have a lawyer who is nothing but a partisan advocate and makes no attempts at objective judgments about the best interest or welfare of the child or question the child's judgment.

14. *In re Gault*, 387 U.S. 1 (1967).

15. See this chapter, note 1.

16. *Application of Gault*, 99 Ariz. 181, 407 P.2d 760 (*en banc* 1965).

17. 387 U.S. 1, 41 (1967) (emphasis supplied).

CHAPTER 8: *TOO EARLY, TOO LATE, TOO MUCH, OR TOO LITTLE*

1. G. Gilmore, The Storrs Lectures: The Age of Anxiety, 84 *Yale L. J.*, 1022, 1044 (1975).

2. See Chapter 2, note 8.

3. *Beyond the Best Interests of the Child* (pp. 31, 40, 49).

APPENDIX I: ON CHILDREN KILLED BY THEIR PARENTS

1. These are actual cases. Karen Spencer's case is quoted from *Report Concerning Karen Spencer to the Derbyshire County Council and Derbyshire Area Health Authority* by Professor J. D. McLean (1978).

2. Dept. of Health and Social Security, *Report of the Committee of Inquiry into the Care and Supervision Provided in Relation to Maria Colwell* (London: Her Majesty's Stationery Office, 1974, ISBN 0 11 320596 1).

3. Ann Shearer, The Legacy of Maria Colwell (*Social Work Today*, 10:12, 14, 1978).

4. See note 2 (this chapter).

5. See also Dept. of Health and Social Security, *Report of the Committee of Inquiry into the Provision and Co-ordination of Services to the Family of John George Auckland* (London: Her Majesty's Stationery Office, 1975, ISBN 0 11 320637 2); Scottish Education Department Social Work Services Group, *Report of the Committee of Inquiry into the Consideration Given and Steps Taken Towards Securing the Welfare of Richard Clark by Perth Town Council and Other Bodies or Persons Concerned* (Edinburgh: Her Majesty's Stationery Office, 1975, ISBN 0 11 491246 7).

*APPENDIX II: SUGGESTIONS FOR SOME
                PROVISIONS OF A CHILD
                PLACEMENT CODE*

1. See *Beyond the Best Interests of the Child* (pp. 53–
    64).

2. *Id.* at pp. 40–49 and p. 98, para. 10.5.

3. *Id.* at pp. 17–20 and p. 98, para. 10.3.

4. This provision coupled with Para. 20.3 *supra* is meant
    to replace Para 30.4 of the Hampstead-Haven Code.
    Id. at p. 100 and see *id.* at pp. 65–67.

Index

Smith, S. M., 244

Smith v. *Organization of Foster Families*, 202, 223–24, 260

Amici Curiae Brief for A Group of Concerned Persons, 224, 260

Social compliance, 74

Socialization of child, 9, 203, 227

Social service agencies, 4, 12–14, 17, 43, 134, 144–85; *see also* Child care agencies

Social worker, 14, 18, 35–36, 44, 70–71, 75, 78–79, 144, 147–81, 224

Society

imperfect, 137–38, 211

lack of consensus, 74, 92, 94–95, 100, 109, 133

Solnit, A. J., 197–99, 201

Spanking, 19, 245–46; *see also* Corporal punishment

Spencer, K., 142–43, 186, 266

Spitz, R. A., 199, 228

Standards, *ad hoc*, 16–17

Stanley v. *Illinois*, 202, 234

State

abuse (exploitation) by, 15–16, 75, 191, 196, 234

insufficiently intrusive, 85–90, 133–35

intervention, *see* Intervention

liability of, 85–86, 196, 234

must give parents opportunity to respond, 22–23

as *parens patriae*, 12, 17, 102, 207

should provide: for child

"unwanted" by parents, 97–98; supportive services, *see* Family, supportive services

too intrusive, 79–85, 133–35; *see also* Parental autonomy

violation of family integrity, *see* Family integrity

State ex rel. Scarpetta v. *Spence–Chapin Adoption Service*, 218

State v. *In the Interest of S. M. G.*, 214–15

Status offense, 28, 213–15

Statutes, 13–14, 16–18, 28, 60–61

child neglect, 79–80, 83–84, 101

child placement, 122–23, 212, 236, 238, 265

favoring custodial family units, 206, 231–32

health care, 101, 103

vagueness, 66, 72, 75, 210, 214, 249

Sterilization of child, 257

Stone, O., 217

Story, Chief Justice, 11

Strauss, 259

Stump v. *Sparkman*, 257

Supreme Court, 46, 204, 210, 215, 234, 258–59

Suspended judgment, 23, 113, 211

Swanson, D., 238

Sweeney, Judge Michael, 251

Tagiori, L., 239

Testo, Judge, 107–08